THE TIES THAT BIND

Miriam Ilgenfritz

Enjoy!

Jam 3:22-23

Miriam Ilgenfritz

authorHOUSE®

AuthorHouse™
1663 Liberty Drive
Bloomington, IN 47403
www.authorhouse.com
Phone: 1-800-839-8640

First published by AuthorHouse   6/15/2010

ISBN: 978-1-4520-1308-4 (e)
ISBN: 978-1-4520-1306-0 (sc)
ISBN: 978-1-4520-1307-7 (hc)

Library of Congress Control Number: 2010907600

Printed in the United States of America
Bloomington, Indiana

This book is printed on acid-free paper.

The Ties That Bind
To my husband Mark, without whom this book would never have been possible.
And to Seth, Lindsay, Benjamin, Rachael, Josiah, Hannah, Naomi, Noah, Esther, David, Elijah, Jedidiah, Ephraim, Moriah, Hosannah, Jerusha, Emmanuel and Stephen who have all helped to prove that truth is sometimes stranger than fiction.
And also, to our parents who, while they didn't always understand why we had all these children, never stopped supporting us in their prayers and countless other ways.

Contents

It has been said, "There are two kinds of truth. True things that are and true things that are not, but could be"

Lest any of you wonder into which category the following narrative falls, these are things which actually did happen.

Prologue

My husband, Mark and I live on a small farm in Central Pennsylvania where we have been blessed with pigs, cows, chickens, golden retrievers and a large quantity of children. Currently we have sixteen. Probably most people that we meet would say our home is full but even with sixteen children, I am not so sure. There is always room for another.

It has been said the kitchen is the heart of the home. In this home, the counters are cluttered with the miscellaneous treasures of sixteen children: a diaper bag, several well-used piano books, and a back pack, sometimes even a tennis shoe or two. There are children of many sizes running in and out. Ephraim who is ten is trying to pour soda from a large bottle into a smaller one. He is concentrating intently as soda is dribbling down the outside of the bottle and puddling on the table Right now Mark, my husband, is cutting Josiah's curly hair. Naomi, the resident artist, is painting a set of Matreshka dolls. Hosannah (eight) is yelling "toot, toot" and pulling Emmanuel (four) around and around our seventeen foot table in a 'boat' made from a laundry basket with a shoestring tied on it. Jedidiah and David are looking at a toy catalog and compiling their birthday wish list. Benjamin is intently practicing Fur Elise on the piano while Hannah can be heard from the living room playing her violin as Jerusha is twirling around and around in her ballerina skirt. Moriah, who is nine, is in the hallway jumping off the fourth step and yelling" three-two-one-blast-off!" He's pretending to be a rocket and I am wondering why it is so quiet in here until I realize that three children are outside and one is napping.

Upon meeting us for the first time, people usually ask" How do you do it?" Now I'm not always sure what "it" is so I sometimes answer 'use duct tape', but family togetherness is one of the ties that hold us together.

In some places, men gather at the local barbershop to shoot the breeze. Our family has found a better way. With 11 boys in our house, the cost of barbering everybody once would keep us in Frosted Flakes for at least six months. However, we have Super Dad. Not even a one year old's screaming protestations are too much for my husband. Flat-tops, buzzes, teddy bears, he is a master of many styles.

We all gather in the kitchen of an evening. The best haircuts are those done first while Dad is fresh so there is some jockeying for who gets the first trim.

The rest of us try to look as if we are cooking or doing dishes or some other worthy pursuit, but the real value here is togetherness. The children and I all watch and comment on each boy's progress. If the night gets late, one of the boys may get a Mohawk or some other unusual cut which Dad will fix in a day or two.

We talk about the day – what work was finished or unfinished. I need to know if the homework is done. We discuss what projects we should try to get done next week and we reminisce about past events. It's a time to reconnect. Everyone gets to voice his or her opinions – an open forum so to speak.

The girls make out the best as they rarely have to sit in the barber chair. We all have fond memories of barbering through the years – Josiah hiding under the bed, Ephraim screaming because he hated haircuts, Benjamin with clay in his hair when Mark was in the pottery years and the times he cut hair out in the yard and then did some of the neighbor men as well. These monthly and bi-monthly gatherings are part of the glue that holds our family together.

The other two events where we all consistently gather involve the supper table and family devotions. Both have also evolved into places where we share the good, the bad and the ugly and bounce ideas off each other.

Sit back in your easy chair now and join us for some of the tales we tell around the barber chair.

Mark, the barber giving Benjamin a trim

1.

One to Remember

Today I was quietly folding wash at the kitchen table. As my table is 17 feet long, there is plenty of room to stack all the piles of clothing. A few children were also gathered, originally doing school work, but now they were distracted by a discussion of their favorite holidays. My favorite holiday might just be Mother's Day, not because it is a day for honoring my role as mother of this brood but because it seems to be the holiday that offers the most opportunity for humor in my house.

Here is the story of my favorite Mother's Day:

It's too bad that Mother's Day always falls on Sunday. For some reason, I had overslept that morning and wasn't quite cognizant of the lateness of the hour.

Benjamin, my responsible 16 year old, awakened by a need to visit the bathroom, knocked on my door. "Mom, aren't we going to Church today?" he queried. I pushed my disheveled hair out of my eyes and glanced at the clock. Well, there would be no breakfast in bed this Mother's Day! But then again, that had never happened anyway. Fortunately we were blessed with a wealth of Cheerios. Some of the children began eating while Seth, our first born, made the rounds of beds that were still inhabited. Soon everyone was gathered around the table slurping milk and reading cereal boxes.

Jedidiah, the ever-thoughtful child, suddenly realized that he had made a present in school for me. Clad in his usual morning attire of baggy T-shirt sporting a gecko in Hawaii, droopy underwear and "Tigger" slippers, he left the table and bolted upstairs to retrieve it. Soon he reappeared with a wrapped box which he presented to me. As I unwrapped the box, Elijah, his seven year-old brother, suddenly realized that Jed had used his box to wrap this gift. With deft and practiced fingers, I ripped the paper off, opened the box, extracted the gift and handed the box to the shrieking Elijah. Pacified, he ran off.

This gift was a piece of artwork bearing a six year-old's hand print and a lovely literary piece about the lasting value of fingerprints on walls. There were quite a few of these stored in the attic already, but I thanked Jedidiah graciously and Elijah returned.

With great anticipation and a sense of precious minutes fleeting past, I opened the box again, only to be greeted by wails from Noah. The gift that Elijah had carefully and thoughtfully chosen for me, his mother, was actually a wildlife notebook belonging to Noah and was never intended for a Mother's Day gift.

Elijah ran out to seek for matching socks while I returned the notebook to the still outraged Noah. After all, what would I do with a wildlife notebook anyway?

As the gift giving appeared to be over and there were still farm chores to do, we decided to leave the dirty dishes on the table to be washed after church. The big boys ran out to feed the animals and the big girls and I looked frantically for socks that had mates, underwear that was clean and pants with no holes in the knees.

Finally all the children were dressed and loaded into the van for the hour drive to church. I had even managed to array myself in a new dress in honor of the occasion.

The van fell silent and everyone breathed a sigh of relief. Maybe, I thought to myself, we won't be late – until Esther yelled "Mom, Hosannah's throwing up all over"

My husband, Mark, pulled into the closest driveway and turned around while the children made all the expected comments:

"EEEEu, gross"

"It stinks back here"…

Hosannah was prone to be car sick so I took her in to change her clothes when David of the small bladder, suddenly decided to use the bathroom. In his rush, he leaped out of the van, fell on the stone driveway and skinned both his knees.

Now Dad was required too. I changed Hosannah's clothes while Mark was Dr. Dad and repaired the knees.

2

Everyone loaded up again. The Ilgenfritz's will be late, but church is not to be missed.

It's not easy to sneak 16 children into church without being noticed. The singing of a hymn is the best time as everyone is standing and we are not quite so obvious. On Mother's Day, church always seems fuller so we had to slink unobtrusively up to the only remaining places which were in the front row. All went well, with only a few obvious glances thrown our way but then Hosannah revealed that she was more than car sick and proceeded to throw up all over my new dress.

Needless to say, at least one of us was required to run out of church with a crying three year old and since I was already messy, I was elected. Meeting my husband in the lobby where my daughter and I had waited for the conclusion of the service, he greeted me by saying,

"Hey, Honey, how about we have someone over for lunch today. Wouldn't that be fun?"

The only thing for me to do was to laugh, gather all my blessings around me and wonder if our potential guests would be satisfied with scrambled eggs on paper plates.

As we drove home, I relaxed in my seat and thought back over the morning. No, it hadn't gone at all as I would have wanted and yet, somehow, it was still a reminder of what a blessing it is to be a mother.

The whole crowd camping in 2006. Back row – Mark, Seth, Esther, Hannah, Benjamin, David, Noah, Naomi and Josiah Front row: Miriam, Hosannah, Moriah, Ephraim, Elijah, Emmanuel, Jerusha and Jedidiah.

2.

Who Are All these People and What are They Doing in My House?

I have heard more than one minister mention that God has a sense of humor and perhaps that is how Mark and I came to meet, fall in love, get married and eventually become the parents of sixteen lovely children. We met in Bible College where Mark was an outgoing soccer player and I was a rather introverted studious young lady thinking that I was either going to go to law school after I graduated or become a single lady missionary. Don't ask how those two interests are related because I have no clue.

Our junior year in college we began dating and soon – six weeks to be exact, we were engaged. We got married that summer, June of 1982 and returned to finish college as married students. Our year was filled with adventures mainly caused by a lack of money which led to learning how to do without.

Our next door neighbors owned a large wood- sided ranch style home which we spent a whole summer scraping and priming and painting all for the huge sum of $600.00 and then we took our lump of cash, packed a small tent and a mattress in the back of our Volkswagen beetle and headed down the road to the Black Hills and Mount Rushmore.

This was my first camping experience and it came complete with car breakdowns and tourist traps and the beginning of a large stash of memories as a married lady. We also became close friends with another young poor married student couple. The husband worked for a bakery so we often enjoyed the goods that were thrown out after the day was over and also laughs when something unpleasant like mold in the lemon filled doughnut were encountered.

The second year of our marriage, we discovered a baby was on the way. This opened the door for all sorts of new excitement as we anticipated our family increasing in size.

After Seth arrived, we moved back to the Pennsylvania area where my husband was born and raised and I gave myself over to the challenge of raising a family. Seth was followed fourteen months later by Benjamin and the adventure was underway.

God provides, generously, for our needs. We started life in Pennsylvania in a little townhouse in Dallastown. Mark was working for a local electrical contractor and I went to school part time, to finish my Elementary Education Degree. After working for close to a year we were no further ahead so Mark came home one day and announced he had decided to go into business for himself. Before Ben was born we had moved into York, to Philadelphia Street. We lived on the first floor of an apartment owned by Mark's Uncle David. The business took off. The first week we were self employed, another cousin of Mark's called and had all sorts of electrical work as they were expanding the plant of which he was vice –president. This got us going. The day Mark told me he was starting on his own; I had just spent the last of our money on diapers and maternity clothes, expecting more paychecks. God had this all under control and we didn't miss a payment on anything.

After another year, we weren't satisfied with our apartment. We looked and looked and finally, just down several blocks, we found a house for sale owned by a little old lady. She sold it to us on condition that she could live there for up to two more years while waiting for her home in the elderly apartments. We put our office in the back and I could walk over to do the bookwork and take Seth and Benjamin along.

By the time Myrtle moved out, Josiah was on the way. This was a big old house and we began fixing it up room by room. The night Josiah was born, we were still finishing up the bathroom and Mark was hoping I wouldn't need to go to the hospital before he finished hanging the tile board. The timing was propitious and I came home from the hospital to a new bathroom.

Not a year later, I was sicker than I could have imagined before and surprise, surprise, Hannah and her twin were on the way. I didn't know it was twins and as I lay on the sofa in the living room with three small boys barricaded in with gates so I could see their mischief without getting up,

I probably didn't care. One twin miscarried but God spared Hannah and she joined us before Seth was five years old followed less than a year later by Naomi. Then we had five kids six and under.

Suddenly it was time to rethink life. Perhaps five children were enough. Maybe we should even consider doing something "permanent". Before we could mess up our lives too badly, God sent someone to help us reconsider. A couple we were friends with invited us out for dinner. We spent the evening visiting and talking about the Lord. To be truthful, I can't even remember what specifics but when we came home we had both come separately to the same conclusion. We needed to trust God for the children He had for us. The rest is history. From five we went to six and so on until we have currently been blessed with sixteen children. To each of you children I would write a note I copied out of Max Lucado's book The Applause of Heaven

> "You were knitted together,
> You were not an accident,
> You weren't mass-produced,
> You were deliberately planned,
> You were specifically gifted,
> and lovingly positioned on this earth by a
> loving father
> and a master craftsman."

I originally started to write this collection of thoughts for my children just to help them remember life in Dornsife, but as it got bigger and bigger I thought perhaps I should write it to show how ordinary parents can do this big job, not by ourselves, but by the grace of God. It is not scary but exciting.

Any sort of introduction I make will be outdated before any of you children read this but I suppose I must start somewhere.

Stephen is the most unknown quantity in our house. At 20 months, he is still developing his personality. Besides being very cute and chubby, he loves music and will sing and dance whenever he hears some lively music. Even as a newborn, he would stop crying if Esther would set his car seat by the piano and play for him. I suppose the saying "music has charms to calm the savage beast" has some truth to it. He also has a temper and doesn't hesitate to let us know if his will is crossed. Stephen is the first baby we ever let sleep in our bed and he is a bed hog. He will lay in the middle with one hand stretched out to either side to make sure Mom and Dad are there but don't get too close and don't cover him up either . He will kick until he is coverless and then fall fast asleep while we shiver on either side of him.

Emmanuel is five. He would dearly love to be as old as any of his big brothers. When I took him to have his kindergarten test, he said, Mom, I'm ready for 1st grade, not kindergarten. Actually, I am ready for the last grade. What do you call it?" I told him Noah was in 12th grade. "Yes" he replied, "I should be in 12th grade." He has a sense of humor too. The other day, I was changing Stephen's very poopy diaper. Emmanuel walked by "Oh my goodness" he said," I can't believe you would do that to your own muvver"

Jerusha has always been my dancing girl. If there are ribbons and lace involved in an activity she is there. If it's pink or purple or in any way related to ballerinas, she will be nearby. The quintessential girl. When she was small she was so cheerful and full of laughter, I almost thought she was too happy. Seven years have sobered her a little but not much. She is like a little Naomi as if the years had folded up and Naomi were back for a time.

Hosannah is nine. She is in many ways, the opposite of Jerusha. A tomboy whenever opportunity arises, probably due to the fact that she has five brothers immediately older than she is and there is a need to not let any of them surpass her. She is very competitive but also very willing to help bathe or diaper Stephen or do other "mommy" type jobs.

Moriah is eleven. A man of opposites. He can annoy everyone around him or be the most tenderhearted little guy. He also spends hours at night lying in bed thinking up questions. Whenever I pass his door on an errand or tucking in someone else, he calls out with another question. He is usually outside, digging up stuff. He has found Indian paint pots, trilobite and worm fossils and all sorts of things in our backyard and is contemplating archeology or marine biology. He is fascinated with the ocean and can't wait until our annual trip to Assateague Island.

Ephraim is about to become twelve. He is the sensitive one. His brothers tease him because he has such a tender heart but some day his wife will be glad that he is sensitive. He is the only one of the children who wears glasses so I can easily tell him apart although he is constantly destroying them doing the things boys do.

Jedidiah is my latest teenager. He is noted for being born between two big blizzards with a total accumulation of over 40 inches. The children have been waiting in vain for similar snowfalls every winter. Jedidiah has been fascinated with cows since he was very small and has his own heifer, Clover.

Elijah is fifteen. I sometimes think he will grow up to be a preacher. He loves the outdoors and anything related to hunting, fishing or camping out. If he had his way, school would be conducted outdoors and consist solely of survival training.

David will be sixteen in two weeks. To define him in one word, I would probably say enigmatic. He does not always express himself as vociferously as some of the other children. When he was small, he sometimes sat at the far end of the table and we forgot to send his plate down to him. Some of the children would have immediately spoken up loudly and demanded their food. David sat quietly on his end and wept but didn't tell anyone. Since he has reached teenager boyhood with its accompanying hunger pangs, we have not had this problem.

Esther is soon to be eighteen. She is the organizer. The year Mark and I went on a cruise for our 25th anniversary, she had the children out of bed at 7:00am to pull weeds in the garden and every meal planned. This was before she was sixteen. She would love to open her own café. Esther loves people and has a heart to minister to others.

Noah, eighteen is our very own rocket scientist. For years he has been building rockets and launching them in the back 40. He also builds fireworks and surprisingly enough, I have never had to worry about him blowing himself up as he is 'very" careful. He is also the only one around here with the distinction of being allowed to own a motorcycle. Currently he is planning to take on-line classes in criminal justice and help us build a new house – but that belongs in a different book.

Naomi is 20 and in her first year of art school. She has enjoyed this year but is looking forward to going to Italy to study art next February, if God wills. She has been working on some smaller commissioned work over this summer to help pay her school bills and add to her Italy fund.

Hannah is 21 and is seeking God's will while she studies nursing. Her heart's desire is to honor God and bring Him glory however that may take place in her life. She is hoping to make a trip to India to check out the health care needs there.

Josiah is 22 and preparing for his 5th year at LeTourneau University. He is studying mechanical engineering and only time will tell where God wants to use him.

Benjamin, 24 is newly wedded to Rachael (Bell) and they have just had their first baby, Joshua Benjamin in Sept. They live just down the road but are anticipating a move to California where Benjamin would like to attend Bible School. Up to this point, Benjamin has worked full time for us as an electrician so this will be an exciting adventure for him, but he and Rachael are learning that when God says "Go," you must be willing to go.

Seth is 25 and married to Lindsay. They are the parents of Jackson and Thomas Houston, who arrived in August. Seth is in his fourth year of medical school and is contemplating the mission field at some future time. Seth was always the trend setter. A short excerpt from his autobiography (written when he was in junior –high) will give a glimpse into his personality.

"Born in a tuxedo, Seth dazzled the world from the beginning. It was obvious at the start that this was no ordinary child: he banged his head so many times while learning basic motor skills that his parents were just hoping that he would live to his second birthday. However, as he came to terms with himself in relation to the world around him, Seth's uniqueness began to manifest itself. On one occasion, after a walk in the park with his nurse, cook, butler and personal servants (namely his parents) Seth looked intently at the ducks. In another instance, he managed to drop himself on his head while his distracted mother was trying to pay for groceries. Anyone who saw him realized that this was no ordinary child. For five years he trained vigorously, mastering skills that he would need to fulfill his purpose in life. Finally, having learned the complexities of Velcro, though not quite how to tie his shoes, Seth set off to accomplish his goal in life: to battle the sinister kindergarten girl gang. Unfortunately, he lost and dragged himself home, bloodied and bruised from having been chucked over a desk in the final confrontation with his nemeses."

Time will tell if Jackson follows in those footsteps, but he seems to be lively guy already at the ripe old age of one.

The Shorter Westminster Catechism states, "The chief end of Man is to glorify God and enjoy Him forever." I sincerely hope our family will achieve that goal and my prayer is that this collection of tales about us will also glorify God.

The super giant snowman

3.

Bingo and the Shopping Mall

An occasional form of entertainment around our house is a trip to the Susquehanna Valley Mall. It begins like this:

Mark, my spontaneous husband says, "Let's do something fun tonight. We could all play a game."

Due to the wide spread ages and abilities of our children, Bingo is about the only game we have found that we can all play together.

Seth, - who is not all that fond of Bingo- replies "We can't play. We've lost most of the pieces."

This is no hindrance to my husband. He just smiles at me, knowing my love of shopping, and says "Let's all get dressed and go to the mall. We'll get a new Bingo game."

This conversation most often takes place around 6:30 or 7:00 pm and the mall closes at 9:00pm. It is also half an hour away. Like toy snakes sprung out of a can, the children all bounce out of their seats and rush around frantically looking for shoes and socks that match, washing faces and hands, combing hair and in general trying to look respectable before we venture out into the public eye. Finally we are all in the van and count heads to insure that everyone actually made it into the car and we set off.

It is an unwritten law in our house that you cannot go to the mall or anywhere else on the "strip" until you visit Lowes' first. I am pretty sure my husband made that rule.

The second stop is Kay Bee toys. Now it is not possible to just walk into Kay Bee toys with a small crowd of children, buy a Bingo game and leave. The proper method is to first walk up and down all the aisles and peruse the entire inventory of the store.

Moriah rides on Seth's shoulders exclaiming "I want that---my birthday," over and over again while other siblings express their desires more maturely.

"Pu-leeeze Daddy, I'll pay you back when we get home, I promise."

"Dad, Dad, you gotta come over here"

And similar sentiments echo throughout the store. Finally we locate and purchase the Bingo game we have come for. On our way out of the mall, we almost always see somebody that we know. This requires a pause in our forward momentum. Those who know the other shopper (Dad) stand and visit while those who are not as social (Mom) try to keep all the children in sight as they mill around among the crowds.

We are like a mall display: "Look but don't touch" People stop to count us and ask us, "Don't you know how this happens?"

"Don't you have television?"

And other penetrating questions. Finally we get close to the store where we entered the mall and the refuge of our van is close outside. Suddenly a large display of Cracker Jack boxes catches Mark's eye. OF COURSE! We need Bingo prizes.

I shepherd everyone to the van while Dad purchases the requisite prizes. We had planned on going out for ice cream but everyone is tired of being a spectacle so we simply stop at the grocery store, buy a Texas pail of ice cream, lots of toppings and have our ice cream at home.

A rousing game of Bingo – Elijah, Seth, Lindsay, Mark and Josiah in hot competition

4.

This Is Not the Man I Married

One of things that changed our life most significantly happened so many years ago that over half of our children weren't even born yet and so have no recollection other than overhearing us talk about it every now and then. At the time, Mark was the owner of York Electrical Contracting, a prosperous business operating from our home on East Canal Road in York, PA.

At one point we had 8 employees and several vehicles on the road to keep up with the electrical work. Our income was more than sufficient even for six children and I was in charge of tax returns, payroll etc, As the days passed , full of everyday occurrences, we began to talk over how it was becoming easy to not have to trust God. We began praying that God would bring us back to a place where we put our trust in Him, not the electrical business. Thus I learned to be careful what I pray for.

One Saturday, Mark had a service call to Chi Chi's Restaurant, a local Mexican place that we did work for. "I'll bring lunch back with me" he told us as he drove off. This was a treat so everyone was excited.

We waited till noon and then till 1pm and then longer and longer until finally I decided either it was a bigger problem than originally thought or Mark had gone on to some other project and lost track of time. After several hours of waiting, I fed the children lunch and then I got "the call." This was a nurse at York hospital and her job was to call and reassure me.

She said," Your husband is here at the hospital. He was in an accident but I can't really tell you anything else"

Well that's quite reassuring. Now I had a houseful of small children and I didn't know if I should drive to the hospital or what.

The God of miracles was still in control. Next thing I know, my brother in law called and told me that he brought a friend in to the ER for a stomach ache and while there, he accidentally saw Mark's name on the admissions list that is supposed to be confidential. Nothing is confidential to God though. Jonas inquired of a nurse and, after denying that he had a brother in law, Mark remembered, yes he does and Jonas brought him home. The Chi Chi's food came too but it wasn't in very good shape anymore. There was a four car pile up when a lady stopped on a windy country road where cars are known to drive swiftly, to pick up a turtle and move it off the road so it wouldn't get squished. She saved the turtle but caused the three cars behind her to pile up. Mark was in the middle of the three and had a closed head injury. We didn't realize the full extent of the problem immediately because there was no visible injury but he couldn't ell time, he couldn't remember the value of numbers and as the week went on, we both realized that something serious had occurred.

After some distress and frustration at figuring out what exactly happened, Mark was an out patient at a local rehab hospital for eighteen months, we had to sell our business, Mark went on disability income and we discovered the only way we could survive financially was to depend on God which is where we should have been all along. The process of figuring out what was next took awhile but through it , we moved to Dornsife where we have lived now for fifteen years, several more children were born to us (ten to be exact), we farmed for awhile and then as Mark's memory improved, God opened the door for him to do electrical work again.

There are some things that will never be the same, and I do think, every now and then that this is not the man I married, but this is the man I am committed to, for better or worse and so together we are raising our family. With the vision that no matter what may happen to either of us, God has a plan for each of these children and He will sustain them. He never promised to provide an amount per family, but His promises are for each individual. When we had one child, we lived in a small apartment. Now that we have sixteen, God has brought us to a small farm in an ideal place to raise all these children but we didn't need that 20 years ago.

We have gone from prosperous small business owner to disabled and unemployed, back to small farmers, gone through a bankruptcy and are small business owners again and God has led us every step of the way. It really doesn't matter how many children you have. If God is providing your means, He provides for everyone. He surely will not cease giving you your needs because you had more than 2.5 children.

We have always lived life on the edge, never knowing what next week would hold and time and time again God has proven Himself faithful to us. I do not always like this process. The times when the next step is hidden in fog and we can see nothing beyond today are frustrating even while I know that God will come through. This week someone wants to buy our farm which may be a very good move for us but we have no idea where we would go and while it seems very clear that God is moving and opening yet another chapter in our lives, He keeps us on a "need to know" basis. Perhaps this is what has developed patience in me more than my sixteen offspring. In any case, as the next chapter opens, I can only recall Mark's words, repeated many times throughout the last 27 years. "It's exciting!"

Displaying their catch: Benjamin, Grandpa and Noah in the back Moriah, Ephraim, Elijah and David in front

5.

Rites of Spring

Nothing says spring more succinctly at the Ilgenfritz house than the advent of Trout Fishing.

The smell of budding trees, small woodland flowers and leaf mold, the last tiny clumps of snow clinging to the undersides of fallen logs or hiding in shadowy patches, the fresh yellow-green of new growth, the sound of a rushing mountain stream and the startled yelp of a boy falling into icy water all combine to remind me of that most cherished event – the first day of trout fishing. Izaak Walton wrote, "God never did make a more calm, quiet, innocent recreation than angling."

Since my husband and I have been married and children began to appear, the trout fishing ritual has been refined and polished to an art. We now have ten boys eligible to participate in this annual festivity. It is also a rite of passage since attendance is limited to sons who are out of diapers. Dad doesn't do diapers. Therefore, the precocious may get to participate at the age of two, but more than likely it will be three.

Trout fishing takes place at an uncle's cabin in the Laurel Mountains of Pennsylvania. The first step is to pack the food. Cereal, bologna, eggs, and all sorts of goodies are all packed up by the three oldest boys. At their ages, food is important and they make sure there's plenty of it. Also packed are long underwear, hats, gloves (it's April) and a change of clothes for all the small guys because someone usually falls in the stream.

Next is the task of procuring bait. Sometimes canned corn is enough but many of the boys hold to the view summed up by Henry Van Dyke who said "The reason life sometimes seems dull is because we do not perceive the importance and excitement of getting bait." Fortunately, we live on a farm and April is sufficiently muddy to locate worms for an army.

Finally, a whole host of fishing rods, tackle boxes, waders, nets and all the other necessary paraphernalia we have accumulated over the years are loaded into our van.

The trip itself is uneventful. It is a two- hour drive unless the boys are fortunate enough to get Dad to stop at a sporting goods store for waders or a license or canned corn. Then a shopping adventure is an added bonus.

When they reach the cabin, the boys have numerous complaints about the rodent tenants who have spent the winter between the sheets of unaired beds and left behind their calling cards. As they grow older, they have discovered that it is a wise choice to bring your own sleeping bag.

There is an old fisherman's saying that, "Nothing grows faster than a fish from the time he bites until the time he gets away." This has been proven true at the cabin as well. Sometime in the afternoon or evening, Great-uncle Dave and several other men show up. Then there are tales of years gone by and the inevitable stories of amazing fish escapes, and finally the restless sleep of those possessing the certain knowledge of this year's big catch.

Trout fishing begins early. Everyone has a hearty breakfast and grabs the specially packed lunch that Grandma has sent along before heading out to select a hole before daylight. With a little luck, someone will catch their limit before lunch, sending everyone else into fervor of casting and reeling in and unwinding small boy's lines from trees. In recent years our second son, Benjamin has become an expert on helping little ones get lines untangled, perhaps reminiscent of the years he was small. If no one falls in, lunch is eaten on the bank with the rough bark of the logs digging into bottoms and the smell of slimy fish on hands.

The essence of the day is summed up by Noah's fish tale: He was about six at the time and as avid an angler as anyone. He had a fine rainbow trout on his line, which he was quite proud of. Actually his big brother Seth had caught it and put it on Noah's hook when he was elsewhere, but Noah was oblivious to this. He reeled it in and his brothers duly admired it.

The trout came home to be viewed by the girls of the family as well and we would have cooked and eaten it but Noah was sent to take his Saturday night bath and unbeknownst to anyone else, he took the trout into the tub with him. The poor thing showed no appreciation for bubble baths.

Finally Noah was persuaded to plant the fish on the hill under some cucumber plants where it may have fertilized them quite well, except he kept digging the plants up to check on the fish

This then is the heart of the trout fishing tradition- not the big catches, but time with family, making memories and stories we can pass down to the next generation. I can picture it now, a room full of little boys and Seth or Benjamin will say, "Have you heard the story of Uncle Noah and the Rainbow Trout?"

And yet another successful fishing expedition: Mark, Seth, Benjamin and Josiah

Stephen enjoying watermelon season to the fullest.

6.

Evolution of the Cheesecake and other Dietary Matters

One question I am frequently asked is:" How do we cook for all these people?"

I usually reply, "Just use bigger pots." Cooking inspires great togetherness. I just need to look like I'm heading towards the oven and I'll have children arguing over whose turn it is to bake. Unfortunately, they don't ever argue over whose turn it is to clean up after the baking session.

Through the years various foods have become specialties at our house. The two highest ranking seem to be lasagna and cheesecake. The lasagna started originally as pizza. The kids have always been big fans of Italian foods. My earliest memories of pizza and children involved Seth Benjamin and Josiah. For a treat we took them to Jim and Nina's pizza for supper. They were so excited. Mom and Dad rarely took them out. The pizza came and they dug in as only toddlers can. We, being indulgent parents, didn't even notice the mess they were making until the couple in the booth just behind us, got up, mumbled something about us making them too disgusted to eat and left the restaurant. Once we got done laughing, we cleaned up the tomato sauce strewn everywhere with our wet wipe supply and didn't eat out for quite awhile after that.

When we moved to the farm, the focus became homemade pizza. We got the proper pizza pans, located a good dough recipe and about once a week we had our own personal all you can eat pizza party complete with cinnamon desert pizza.

The children all liked to get involved. When David was three and Elijah, two, David was sitting in a large pot on my kitchen floor and Elijah had a ten pound bag of flour open all over the floor. When asked what in the world they thought they were doing, they replied, rather surprised, "We're making pizza."

Well you can either laugh or cry. So I laughed and took some photos. As most moms know, this can all happen in the space of time it takes to run to the basement and change the laundry.

Spaghetti was also a common meal due to its ease and using not very many pots. Somehow those two foods transmogrified into lasagna. For almost every birthday, lasagna was the requested meal. When Seth turned sixteen, he got tuxedo lasagna. After that it became a joke that Mom's lasagna was the best and any girl wishing to marry into the family would have to pass the "cook lasagna like Mom" test. Now that two of the boys are married and they never forced anyone to run the lasagna gauntlet, I think this test has gone by the wayside. Since lasagna has been mastered and now even my daughters can make it with ease, I have had to move on to greener pastures, such as desert making.

As the mother of sixteen children, I have had to learn many new and exciting skills. One of my favorites is the art of the cheesecake. Over the past 27 years I have progressed by fits and starts down the path to cheesecake success.

I had always heard that cheesecakes were hard to produce correctly. I have also always enjoyed a creative challenge, so early in our marriage I decided to learn the art to tempt my husband.

My first step was clear – ask my mother. At the time, she was not a cheesecake baker and sent me to the next obvious source – a good cookbook. Once I began reading about these elusive deserts, my curiosity was aroused and I actually started looking into their history. One cookbook writer refers to cheesecake as a result of culinary evolution. It seems that cheesecakes of one sort or another have been around as long as there have been milk-producing animals. Ancient Greeks and Romans have left us recipes for similar cakes to those made today.

Having satisfied my curiosity about how cheesecake came to be, I also found in my studies that cheesecake baking leaves plenty of room for creativity. There are appetizer cheesecakes (one of our favorites is a crab cheesecake for spreading on crackers) there are plain New York Style cheesecakes just waiting for a light delicious fruit sauce to poured over them and there are rich decadent concoctions such as hot fudge cheesecake (not for the diet conscious or faint of heart).

Imagine my surprise when all my children developed a taste for cheesecake. First one and then another would ask for a special birthday cheesecake. Soon their confidence in my abilities began to be frightening as they would ask for cheesecakes I had never heard of. Josiah's favorite request was always pistachio cheesecake and I kept refusing to make one until finally I decided anything is fair game. Let's invent new cheesecakes.

As the years have gone on, cheesecake has become my family's favorite for birthday celebrations and with 18 people under one roof, we have 18 favorite cheesecakes. I have gone from the simple cookbook varieties to making up my own to meet some child's whim.

Our family has now reached the point that I have threatened to write a book entitled <u>101 Things to Do With Cream Cheese</u> or <u>The Way To A Man's Heart Is Through His</u> <u>Stomach</u>. While it might be a best seller, I am too busy thinking up new flavors to write it.

Keeping us all fed has become a major event demanding togetherness and making many memories, most of them fond. We raise several steers and pigs every year. Every year different children are in charge of taking care of various members of the menagerie. This has occasionally backfired. One fall Mark and several of the children attended the Gratz fair where they sold emu burgers to patrons. At the end of the fair, the owner of the petting booth felt that his little pig was too grown up and so we bought her. David was in charge of her. He named her Peaches and spent quite a bit of time with her. She was so cute and friendly and by the time she grew up, David was quite attached. Even though he knew all along that we were planning to eat her, he went almost two years after her demise refusing to eat pork and questioning if this meat came from Peaches or some other family pig. Since then, we have learned not to get too attached to our food. It's better to buy a mean ornery pig than a cute friendly one if you plan to eat it later.

We have learned how to do much of our own butchering. The older boys are quite capable of dealing with a pig all on their own if Dad is busy with something else and once the meat arrives in the house, everyone who can handle a knife without too much danger gets to help prepare the meat for consumption. Most of my kids can clean out a chicken, de bone a pig or deer or help stuff sausage casings. They look forward to our traditional pig day –usually New Year's, as a time where we will spend the day in the kitchen together and even though it's hard, and messy, its part of what makes us a family.

The garden is another area requiring everyone's help and inspiring tales of who did the most or grew the biggest vegetable. The year Hannah was home schooled by herself, she tilled and planted well over half of our huge garden and then helped in the canning and preserving of it. While causing some distress at the actual time of tilling, she later looked back on it with quite a feeling of accomplishment.

Several of our traditional plantings have developed reputations. Red beets are an annual favorite. We eat them freshly pulled, boiled with butter on and they taste like corn on the cob. One year Moriah ate three or four large plates of red beets for supper. While I knew he enjoyed them, this seemed a little excessive so I finally asked why he was so hungry. He said, "Oh, I'm not, I just wanted to pee red at school tomorrow and scare my teacher"

Indeed red beets do have that effect. After we have eaten our fill of fresh beets, we pickle and can them. I need to put away at least 80 quarts of pickled beets to make it through the winter.

Green beans aren't welcomed quite so heartily. While we all like them fresh, there seems to be an aversion to frozen beans and our canned ones take forever in the pressure cooker and don't hold up very well.

Fresh eggs generate a lot of stories. The most memorable one involves the year we built a deluxe chicken coop and invested in 25 buff Orpington hens and a rooster. We stated with peeps and nursed them carefully through the cold spring in our basement while they waited for the coop to be finished. Finally they moved in and began to eat and grow. By the time Father's Day arrived, they were almost ready to begin laying delicious brown eggs. That particular Sunday we had two children from church staying with us which made it even more dramatic when someone discovered our golden retrievers had pillaged the chicken coop. Needless to say, we were late to church and our guests had a few more stories to tell about us when they went home.

Sauerkraut is a perennial favorite. We often plant 70 heads of cabbage and gather everyone in the kitchen to help grate and stomp, grate and stomp until it has all been shredded, salted and then all that is left is the clean up and the long wait till it has fermented properly for us to eat. At that point we roast the biggest piece of pork I can find in the freezer and have a pork, sauerkraut and mashed potato feast.

It is entirely possible that our need to have milk cows began with Jedidiah. When he was around two years old we passed a farm on our way to the grocery store every week. The field next to the road was filled with cattle that seemed to be always lying around chewing their cuds. He was fascinated with these creatures and announced to us one day

"Hey Mom, look at the cows. They're hatching their eggs."

We all laughed at the ridiculous thought, but every week Jedidiah looked for the cattle and when a few young calves were running around he was relieved to see that the eggs had finally hatched.

Since that time we started having cattle on the farm and when Jedidiah was eleven, he became the proud owner of a Jersey heifer that he named Clover. Clover is now expecting her own first calf but while we were waiting for that day we have gone through a gamut of cows.

There was Melissa, also a Jersey but the kids complained that her teats were too small -she was bred for a milking machine. After several months we sold her and looked for another cow. One of our neighbors sold us a cow that we named Lottie because she gave lots of milk but she also kicked so we had to tie a rope around her belly when ever we milked to keep her from kicking the children. She also liked to sleep up in the pine forest. Neither Seth nor Benjamin cared too much to go out at 5:00 AM on a winter morning, hunt for a stubborn cow in the dark, milk her without getting kicked and then get cleaned up before the school bus arrived.

We had Buttercup and Queen Helen as well before Clover arrived. One of our neighbors gave Queen Helen to us to milk as they had more cows than he wanted for awhile. For some reason, no one could stand to drink her milk so finally, feeling rather ashamed, we gave her back. Our neighbor looked a little surprised but then admitted that his children didn't like her milk either.

Our current cows are Buttercup II whom we had to dry up. Buttercup stepped on her teat much to Esther's relief – Esther hates milking and now we have Anne who just gave birth to Strawberry Shortcake so we have fresh milk again while we wait on Clover.

The saga of cows will probably go on for a few more years as it is still cheaper to milk our own than it is to purchase store milk. The kids always come in and say" Is this cow milk?" meaning "raw" and I always answer

"Of course, did you want to drink camel milk?"

Then they sigh and say, "Mom, is it from the store?"

Some of them prefer store milk and some raw, but with raw milk we can include real butter, unlimited yoghurt, homemade ice cream and even cream cheese in our diets and most of the time this method is preferred as long as you aren't the child designated as the milker tonight.

All in all, we eat well and frequently and the process has given us many memories and family stories.

One of our favorite summer meals – steamed blue crabs

7.
Road Kill Café

Possum Stew

One recently caught possum, skinned and cut into small pieces (you can use road kill scraped off the pavement but be sure it's fresh. If it's covered in flies, don't use it for this recipe. It would be better suited for Possum Hash)
4 medium taters, cubed
3 carrots, sliced thickly
2 ribs celery, sliced thickly
1 medium onion
2 cloves garlic, minced
3 cans stewed tomaters
4 slices bacon
Salt and pepper to taste

Cook bacon slices in heavy, deep pot until crisp. Remove bacon and crumble. In reserved bacon drippings, cook onion and garlic until tender. Add tateres, carrots, celery, cans of tomaters, salt, pepper, bacon, and possum meat. Bring to boil. Lower heat, cover and simmer on low for 4 hours. Enjoy with a nice jug o' moonshine.

Ever since we have been married, we have occasionally resorted to a manner of getting food affectionately known to my children as The Road Kill Café. It is important to understand that we are very particular about our menu. There are certain rules governing the Café and the items that can be served.

First of all, the animal in question must be a commonly edible one. I draw the line at squirrels and opossums even though they are edible. Fresh venison will make the menu; opossum pie is a café faux pas. Secondly, I must be able to ascertain how recent of a tragedy the proposed item is. If it can be proven fresh, it can be brought home and eaten. I suppose this rather callused view of life comes from living on a farm at the foot of a mountain. Deer on the road are seen frequently and if one has been hit, why waste perfectly good meat.

The other contributing factor to our use of the Café is the fact that we already do our own butchering on the farm so if its winter and cold out, a fresh deer is not that big a deal to skin and clean and we all enjoy a freshly grilled tenderloin.

One year my niece and nephew from Chicago came for a visit. On the way home from church we passed a deer that had not been there on the trip down so we knew it was only an hour old. Pulling over quickly, Mark and Seth threw it in the back of our van and we drove home. I made a fast lunch and instructed the children to change quickly so we could skin the deer out before it got too warm. Imagine my surprise when my city born and raised relatives weren't hungry for supper. This was a completely new way of finding food and didn't even come close to grocery shopping.

The children are also familiar with the fact that on a farm, there are always animal tragedies and if an animal meets an untimely end that is not due to illness, it will get eaten. So one day I discovered that the bedroom window in the little boys' room was open. This room is three stories up and a fall from there would probably be fatal. I could hardly believe that someone would dare to open it, much less leave it open so I could find it. I rushed in, in a panic and yelled "I can't believe you guys opened this window! Don't you know what would happen if someone fell out? They would be dead."

Ephraim was about four at the time and he looked at me with his very serious face and said, "It's okay Mom. Couldn't you just eat them?"

Hot dogs in Maine

8.

The Stuff of Memories

"It always rains on tents. Rainstorms will travel thousands of miles, against prevailing winds for the opportunity to rain on a tent." ~Dave Barry

In winter, when hair is being cut, it is a good time to dream of next year's vacation. This always means we have to first reflect on all of our past camping trips.

The rain lashed our tent in the darkness like sharp spikes while the wind threatened to tear the stakes out of the sandy ground. My husband and I glanced at each other in consternation, while our half- cooked chicken dinner drowned on the grill just outside the tent flap. Eventually we assigned one of our big kids to run out every half hour to check the stakes and finally, we put our sleeping bags on top of the picnic tables which were under our large cooking tent. Then we huddled together and tried to sleep as the water rose around us.

Hardly an auspicious beginning to the first night of a long- anticipated camping trip to Assateague Island, Maryland, with fourteen children, and yet, these are the very things that memories are made of.

In this world of fast-paced technology and instant gratification of any desire, why in the world do we still insist on camping? My theory is that adversity develops closeness. When our children grow up and reminisce with each other, their vacation memories will be a large part of their conversations because we remember the challenges. Try it; you too may become addicted to challenging adversity.

Camping is a wonderful way to work together through a challenge and make some great memories. It is also inexpensive and even as a larger family, we can afford to travel once we have trained the children how to put up tents.

Camping Just the mention of the word brings uncountable memories. Just how did all this camping nonsense get started anyway? As a child, my parents didn't camp. People who camped were our neighbors in their pop-up or maybe my cousins who regaled us with tales of their adventures, but not us. We hiked and explored and went on vacation, but never camped.

Suddenly I was a married woman and the first opportunity we had to go on vacation, Mark decided we should camp. We loaded a small tent, a mattress, two sleeping bags and a few clothes into an old VW beetle and headed across Minnesota to the Black Hills of South Dakota. We didn't even bother to make reservations anywhere, just stopped when the mood hit us and after repairing whatever had broken on that day's drive, we set up our tent. That is, Mark set up the tent and I tried to help and learned about how not to put up a tent. We had a wonderful week and then the children began making their appearances and we didn't camp for quite awhile. After we had seven children, the bug hit again. This time we began small. There were many nights when we draped covers all over our huge living room and built "tents" for the children. This wasn't too scary since they didn't have to leave the house.

Once the boys got a little bigger, they began camping out every now and then in the backyard with their daddy. We would put up a tent, build a campfire, roast hot dogs and marshmallows and then I would bring the babies in to sleep while Mark slept out with the boys.

After we moved to the farm, Mark and the older boys got involved with frontier camping so we invested in a large period canvas tent. The year Hosannah was a baby we took the plunge – a real family vacation. We had always wanted to take a trip to Maine. A borrowed RV was loaded down with provisions and maps and five extra tents to hold all fifteen of us. We had reservations at a campground on Mt Desert Island close to Acadia National Park. What an adventure that turned out to be.

The thirteen hour drive stretched into 24 as we broke down and repaired the RV time after time. This was before the widespread use of cell phones but we were always close to some sort of help. At one point we were on top of Cadillac Mountain and the silly thing refused to start. A fellow tourist asked if he could be of assistance and prayed for our vehicle. It started up and got us back to the campground. That same evening, the owners of the campground offered us the use of their vehicle to run into town for parts and even gave all the children a free pass to miniature golf when we were running again.

The trip home was equally eventful but we always knew God was with us. Since that time, camping has become a favorite activity. Two years later we began camping at Assateague Island National Seashore and it has become a perennial favorite for the children.

For activities encouraging bonding and togetherness, I always recommend camping. The disasters draw you closer together and it's an inexpensive way to be reminded of how much you love each other and how thankful you are to have hot showers when the week is over. What began as a small living room activity has grown and grown to be a major accomplishment of packing and organization but we wouldn't trade it for anything.

We have taken take the camping challenge almost every year now. True to form, the first night that we camp anywhere, a big thunderstorm will blow in. It then becomes necessary to assure all the younger children that even though we are camped on a flat sandy beach, we are probably not the highest spot in the area. Surely someone else's tent stands higher than ours and would attract the lightning.

For mild adversity, but nothing too extreme, I love Assateague Island National Seashore. We put our tents up on the sand dunes and are right on the Atlantic Ocean. There are wild ponies and deer that will travel through our campsite so we have learned to lock our food in the vehicles when not cooking, but the children are thrilled to meet wild ponies face to face. (Don't feed them, they bite). There is no hot water and no flush toilets. We used to think this was bad until we realized that it keeps many campers away and you have an almost private beach to play on. When sunburn hits, we go across the road to the bay and catch crabs for supper, just don't forget the bug spray. Tents are always an issue. Every year we have to prove to the Park Rangers that we really are one big happy family and can legally camp on only two sites.

Since we live close to the East Coast, our destinations have been mainly eastward. We have camped on Mt Desert Island in Maine- this was the RV experience we all recall fondly, on the St Lawrence Seaway, called the 1,000 Islands, which we remember for hauling a pontoon boat on a homemade trailer and having several blown —out tires and a overheating engine, and also for the educational opportunity of meeting the Canadian Border Patrol while out on the boat, and on Assateague Island National

Seashore, in Maryland. Assateague is easy because it is only 6 hours from our home and if time is short, we can do a day or two camp where some of the other places we have traveled require more of a time commitment.

Every year as summer approaches the questions arise: Can we camp this summer? And: Where will we go- a new unexplored destination or an old favorite?

Somewhere on the list are the big destinations: Mt Rushmore, Yellowstone or my favorite childhood spot, the Rocky Mountains in Colorado. These all will require a good bit of planning ahead and we may never make it to them but "without a vision, the people perish". It is good to have some goals, even for our vacations. Our goal has never been to encounter trials. Rather we go to great lengths to avoid them, packing twice as much stuff as necessary and taking up to a week to get ready for a short trip but the nature of camping seems to invite trouble. So the question keeps rising up – why do we camp every year? And I return again to my original premise that adversity brings us closer together: we remember the hard times and they are part of the glue that bonds our family into a family.

The end of a fine day at the beach – no rain in sight

9.

Some Thoughts on Entropy

Back when we had only thirteen children, I was looking for a creative way to write our annual newsletter and what came out was the following detective story.

Case file # 1-39A Willitt O.Willittson here (W.O.W) for short). Private Eye.

This story may not sound true, but this harrowing experience was nearly my last.

It all began one crisp autumn day at my office in rural Dornsife. A rapid knocking sounded, but before I could rise to open the door, it burst open and a blond, disheveled young man, gasping for breath and babbling incoherently met my eyes. The only words I could make out were…"mother, crazy," and "can't find"

I finally convinced the poor fellow to sit down and offered him a glass of water. After he had regained his composure, he told me his tale.

It started last May when the family's socks began disappearing at an alarming rate. This wasn't too bad, because Mr. Ilgenfritz, the head of the home, had a sock condition that caused him to buy new socks every two or three weeks. He also coded the socks "Dad's", "Dad's New", etc. so they wouldn't get lost. Be that as it may, a few weeks ago, when the family was eating breakfast, they noticed that they only had half as many bowls as usual. Then they noticed that no matter how many dishes they washed, there were never enough knives in the drawer. This strange lack of household items was driving their mother nearly to insanity. The straw that broke the camel's back was when she saw that time was never enough. Why just the other Sunday, the youth reported, they noticed that the days were getting shorter. The boy looked at me with fear in his eyes. With thirteen children in the household, this was serious.

I took the case!

My first line of attack to crack this case was to investigate the thirteen children. Children often know much more that they let on, so I would have to be discrete. I decided to start with the youngest children first.

Hosannah was walking around and around the table with a sock in one hand, muttering "Da-DA-Da."

While this seemed a promising suspect, I soon realized that thirteen months was pretty young to steal socks, bowls and knives, not to mention time, so I turned my attention to Moriah.

With his eager smile and bright blue eyes, I thought I'd make progress. He only grinned and said "nite-nite Ben"

This seemed to be his standard response to all the big boys. The only other word I got from him was "NO", but he's two so what else could I expect.

Jedidiah (four) and Ephraim (three) got my attention next. They were coloring pictures at their long table. Jedidiah was drawing lobsters. He's been doing this since he was in Maine in June. Ephraim was scribbling letters to his cousin peter. At the same time, they were singing cow songs and refused to speak with me, a total stranger.

I tracked Elijah (six) down outside, shooting at targets with his bow. Hoping to gain more insight, I implied that he might know something, at which point he ran inside with his blankie, leaving behind a knapsack packed with several socks, a bowl, and a knife, but not enough to warrant this investigation. He later claimed it was because he was going camping.

David (seven) was playing "Away in the Manger" on the piano. He said he knew nothing about socks and his interest was in collecting giraffes. I did notice a copy of <u>Sherlock Holmes</u> on the bench beside him, but paging through it gave me no clues. I also noticed he was wearing tennis shoes with no socks, but I decided to interview Esther as David wasn't very informative.

Esther (eight) was full of information. She could tell me to the exact minute when each missing item was noticed, who was in the room at the time of discovery, and a variety of other irrelevant facts about family members but she had no idea who was guilty. She said she had to practice piano then, and I went in search of Noah (ten).

He was shooting holes in apples with his BB gun and claimed to have no information. I did note that he was wearing socks, and also that he had a large safety pin hooked on his belt loop which is how the Ilgenfritz's keep their socks matched in the wash, but this didn't help my investigation.

I returned to the house where Naomi (eleven) was busy sketching. She had no new information but did volunteer to draw my picture. I've included it with this transcript.

Hannah (twelve) was playing the violin and only smiled at my questions. When she finished her practicing, she disappeared behind the covers of a large book. This left me only three teens to interview.

Josiah (thirteen) had six or seven safety pins on his belt loop, leading me to surmise that he was forgetful about pinning his socks together, but nothing about missing socks, table knives or cereal bowls. He was lying on his bed reading. We talked until his train clock began running around the track. Then he politely dismissed me and returned to his book.

Benjamin (fifteen) was outside building a dam in the stream. He answered many questions about gardening, building as well as hunting and fishing, but not a clue about missing items in their home.

I was stumped. This was the toughest case I'd hit yet. Seth (sixteen) who had sought my help was out in his car practicing parallel parking but I already knew all his information. What was I missing? I decided to talk to Mrs. Ilgenfritz. She was peeling potatoes with one of the few remaining knives and singing softly...

"Socks that are matching, and knives in the drawer,
Swiss Mocha coffee, no towels on the floor.
Floors that are swept, and no missing shoe strings,
These are a few of Mom's favorite things."

I didn't wait to hear the rest of the song. It was clear I could never solve this puzzler. There were simply <u>too</u> many variables. Chalk this one up to experience, I'll pass. As for Mrs. Ilgenfritz – her final words as I left were, "its okay, that's just life with thirteen children."

Whenever life begins going along smoothly, there will be a bump in the road just to remind us that we are dependent on God, not ourselves and force us to turn again to Him.

There is also the fact that nothing ever stays the same. It is constantly wearing down or breaking or descending into chaos.

Last winter I was pretty sure entropy was overtaking us. It started with the dishwasher. We were renovating a house and in the course of working on the kitchen at the new house, a new dishwasher came my way as well. The old one had been subject to random fits of leakage so this seemed a good time to replace it. This appeared to be an easy task but when Mark pulled out the old dishwasher, we discovered that it had been leaking for quite awhile through the floor and into the basement, just not out in front where we could see it. The floor underneath was rotten. Obviously this would be a bigger project than we anticipated at first.

While this project was still in process, our water in the house began shutting off. We have our own well and I am used to running quite a few things in my attempts to multitask. I can have someone in the shower, run two washing machines, the kitchen sink and the dishwasher all at one time without too much distress for the person in the shower. Suddenly I could only use one item at a time and it wasn't going to be the dishwasher. The only way to deal with this problem was run to the basement, shut off the washing machines, turn off the pump, wait a few minutes, reset the pressure switch, run back upstairs and remember to start everything up again.

We were all still fairly cheerful about these things and then the house got cold and then colder. It was January and I don't tolerate cold very well. Since Mark was going out to get plumbing parts, he decided he might as well get some furnace parts too. Then, to take the cake, our old furnace down in the basement sprang an oil leak. Now my husband can fix anything but everything in one week was a little much. Still, one can either laugh or cry. We decided to have a good laugh and then work at fixing one thing at a time. The furnace has been removed, the circulator fixed, the water tank has a new pressure switch and I have a new list of things that need repaired this winter.

Entropy hits us in other areas also. For example, I have a dishwasher, a regular sized kitchen sink and a large three bay restaurant size sink and I still cannot keep up with the demand for clean dishes. Over the years I have become convinced that that at least in our house, dirty dishes breed in the sink at night. No matter how empty the sink is at night, there are more dishes there in the morning. One year I interviewed some of the children to see if anyone knew the answer. Benjamin was seventeen at the time, and he offered the first plausible theory.

"I believe dishes are like Hattifatteners. The multiply especially fast during thunderstorms. Outlets by the sink increase this disposition still more"

This didn't entirely explain my dish problem, so I asked Naomi. She put forward her theory eagerly. "Dishes are relatives to amoebas and they divide asexually at night while no one is looking."

Ephraim and Jedidiah simply said "Mom, eating food makes more dishes."

They wondered why was this was so hard for me to understand. They also added they sincerely hoped I wasn't planning to ask them to help whip the dishes into submission.

The more I think about housework and dishes, the more I become convinced that it is a simple mathematical equation. The degree of cleanliness of your house is a directly proportional ratio of mess created by toddlers and ability and numbers available to clean. In other words, if you have mostly older children, your house will be cleaner than if you have a higher ratio of preschoolers.

On the other hand, no matter how many preschoolers or almost adult children you have, entropy is always out there lurking just beyond the door, waiting to force its way in. My husband is not so romantic about it. He just says, " Everything is either being cleaned up or messed up. There is no in- between"

He is right of course. There is nothing really lurking and conspiring to trash my house. Life is messy and I have come to grips with that. I refuse to give up and let it overtake me but neither shall I let it rule my life. When everything breaks down, its time to gird up my loins and go to work so that when we are done, we'll have another memory in our cache of stories to tell when we are old.

10.

Hay Fever

Hay, Hay, Hay (with apologies to William Shakespeare)
To do hay or not to do hay: that is the question:
Whether 'tis nobler in the mind to sleep through
The wind and rain of a stormy day,
Or to rise up and make hay? To rest: to sleep;
Once more; and by a sleep to say we end the back-ache from
A thousand bales of hay that we would have carried
Today,' tis consummation devoutly to be wish'd.
To rest, to sleep; to sleep perchance to dream: aye there's the rub;
For in that sleep so sweet what dreams nay come when we have
Shuffled off the hay for another day, must give us pause:
There's the respect that makes hay take so long…
Enough with the Shakespeare!

"Get up Naomi, Dad's waiting to make more hay!"
-Naomi Ilgenfritz (@age13)

Every year my husband comes down with a severe attack of hay fever. It hits in May when the weather is fine and the pastures are growing out of control and lasts until the last possible cutting of hay in August or September.

Nothing inspires my children to thoughts of mutiny quite as quickly as the words "Its time to make hay"

They have learned first hand what that little adage "make hay while the sun shines" really means. When everyone was small, our neighbor came over with his equipment and helped us cut and bale the hay. Sometimes Seth and Benjamin were able to help load the bales but as they grew, additional children were big enough to help and so the hay making project grew as well.

I would not call this endeavor a finely tuned process. Usually it is fraught with stress. First of all, the weather has to be cooperative. In May we begin spending a great deal of time on the internet looking at the five and ten day forecasts. There must be enough sunshine for several days to cut the hay, ted the hay, rake the hay, drying time, baling time and time to load it up in the barn before a thunderstorm hits. Add to this the fact that we usually use older equipment and so there are breakdowns and time off to run for parts or see if any neighbors have equipment we can borrow while we are trying to fix ours.

Hay making has led to many tales around the barber chair and fond memories which have been repeated so often they now have names such as the year we had the "Brown Steel Farm Encasement Project". This involved not only hay season, but all the spare time in between, building storage for the hay and covering each building with brown steel to keep out the rain.

Seth's big hay memory probably is the year he turned fifteen. We always said if it was your birthday, you got the day off but that year on his fifteenth birthday, the hay was ready to cut and since he was the oldest he had to help. Since then the age of helpfulness has been lowered to thirteen. Egg sandwiches became popular during hay season. You can fry up the eggs, slap some mayonnaise and mustard on a slab of bread and carry it out to the hay field without much trouble. The only thing you need to remember is who likes mayonnaise and who will only consume miracle whip in their sandwich.

On occasion we cut hay for our neighbors. One year one of our Amish neighbors got behind and asked Mark to come cut some of his hay fields. We mowed and mowed and baled and repaired and baled and repaired some more and then the rain began to move in. Some of the hay was left lying in the fields since no one wants to be out on a metal tractor in a lighting storm. That hay was ruined but it had to be brought in anyway so the new hay could grow. After all that work, the farm was sold that fall, moldy hay and all and we saw no return for all that work. I shouldn't say no return, the kids have learned a great deal about agriculture, hay equipment, and the satisfaction of a good day of hard work. They just haven't realized all that yet. Naomi wrote a poem about hay one year for the newsletter which helped me realize how big hay making figures in their memories.

Another benefit of making hay is the driver education it provides. Quite a few of the children have begun their driving careers either driving the old farm truck or driving our New Holland tractor with equipment on the back. As would be expected, this has occasionally added to the stress factor as our pastures are not flat but hilly and lumpy and require some ingenuity when driving.

It's March as I write this and the grass is just beginning to green. There will probably be a snow or two on it yet and then suddenly it will begin to grow.

Over the winter we got a newer baler than the one we had and a hay bine for better cutting ability and so I called together my older children and said,

" Gird up your loins, a big hay harvest is coming."

I'm pretty sure we are not raising any farmers here in Dornsife but we are learning to work together and we are making some lasting memories of our time together as a family.

Checking out the harvest

Hosannah preparing to press apple cider

11.

The Spinning Bowl
and Other Small Traditions

Some hair cutting stories go on to live in infamy and they do not all involve Mark. Naomi went through a stage in life where her daddy was trying to teach her to cut hair so she could take over on nights when eleven haircuts were a few too many. Noah wanted a haircut and nagged and nagged her to cut his hair. It was fairly obvious that Naomi was not in the hair cutting mood as she kept refusing him, but finally Noah wore her down and she agreed to trim his locks. As the trim went on and advice was being given, somehow Naomi got inspired to trim the eyebrows of her customer. The end result was no eyebrows at all for poor Noah and this tale has gone on to be told again and again whenever someone asks Naomi for a trim. It has joined our collection of small traditions, along with a few others I recall.

If it's breakfast time and I hear the shouted words," That's my bowl." Or, "It was my turn."

Chances are it is a fight over the spinning bowl. Who would have thought that such a small investment in Tupperware would have turned into a family icon? Still, however it happened, I bought a red plastic Tupperware bowl the year I got married and from Seth to Stephen, it has become a favorite and when children serve their own breakfasts, the one most often picked first. Perhaps the attraction lies in the red color, but I am more inclined to think it lies somewhere in the fact that when you fill it with milk and cereal and twirl a spoon in it, you will eventually overcome inertia and encounter a physics law that forces the milk to swoosh out of the bowl and spread itself all over the kitchen table, or a sibling, if you are especially talented.

I have read all sorts of articles and even books on the importance of establishing family traditions. They typically refer to holidays and big events while ours all seem to be small traditions such as a bowl, but important nonetheless for keeping us united. We laugh at our traditions but let anyone outside the family mock them and any or all of us will rise up in defense.

Uncle Johnny is another family tradition. He shows up without warning and only ever stays a few days. He first came around when Seth and Ben were small. Mark shaved his beard off one evening when the boys were in bed already and when they got up the next morning, he spent a great deal of time convincing them that he was not Dad, but Uncle Johnny come to visit. When the beard grew out, Uncle Johnny went away but returns about once a year or sometimes more often to be introduced to the younger children who haven't met him yet. He has completely different behavior than Dad and we all know that Uncle Johnny does not obey the same rules as the rest of us.

The boys have a trout fishing tradition so one year Naomi, Hosannah and Jerusha decided to initiate the Secret Girls Club. This consisted primarily of writing a silly song which they then sang over and over until I can still recite the words from memory and I was never invited to join in the first place.

"I may never eat a baby bumblebee
Jump over a banana tree
Drink a leaky battery
I may never sleep in a pickle tree
But I'm in the S.G.C. Yes sir!"

Other of our traditions involve work. About every other year our well pump goes bad and because it is almost 500 feet under the ground, it requires everyone to help pull the pipe out and lay it on the ground until we reach the pump. Then it must be repaired and worked back down into the well. There is always a unified groan when someone announces "the water's off again"

Seth and Emmanuel pulling out the well

Another work related tradition was started by Hannah. There is a story in several fairy tale books about brownies that work in your house in the night and are happy with the payment of a bowl of milk for their labor. Every now and then on the night before my birthday or Mother's Day or maybe Christmas, the brownies come out and clean up my house after I am in bed. I have not seen them lately, but I am not sure if it is because they have gone off to college or because I haven't left any milk out lately. I think this summer I will leave out some milk and see if my house is any cleaner in the morning.

A fondness for Celtic Music was the fuel for another" almost tradition." I had a vision for our family playing music together, even if it was only at the county fair. Seth built an uillean pipe and then purchased a real one as he improved. He also worked a few years on learning to play the dulcimer. Hannah spent several years working on violin and fiddle music, Esther and Naomi play piano, as well as Josiah and Benjamin, who also invested in a mandolin and bodhran respectively, and I play the flute so we spent a lot of effort trying to get an Irish music group together. The result of that was a familiarity with common Irish tunes and some fun trips to Celtic festivals. We gave our group a name and even wrote up a page about our tour in our annual newsletter as a joke, but everyone finally realized that playing as a group takes more effort than we had time for especially as the children began to go off to college and medical school.

I harbor a secret hope that some year this music thing will still come together but I have ceased holding my breath. It was fun while it lasted and I still have my flute to play and perhaps someday I will learn to play the piano and maybe the harp and maybe a dulcimer or mandolin and maybe when I'm 80 and we have a family reunion, we will attend the Northumberland County Expo and play old songs together for the fair patrons instead of the Elvis Impersonator they have now.

With the coming of age of some of our children, we began to notice a growing concern among various friends and family members regarding the finding of boyfriends and girlfriends. We then established a new tradition – the Courting Practices of the Ilgenfritz's. These ran as follows: first of all, if you were a potential male suitor, you must run the gauntlet, secondly, you would have to pass an interview with the eleven Ilgenfritz brothers – a daunting task considering one of them barely talks yet, and some of the boys still consider marriage a disgusting idea (girls –YUCK). If you were a young lady, there was the 'cook lasagna like Mom " test as well as meeting Mark's strict criteria for wifely readiness. Also, a female candidate would need to be compatible with five very different and unique females who could end up being sisters-in-law. We also advised candidates of both sexes to learn to play an instrument that could be used in traditional Irish music and to cultivate a taste for sea chanties. Since these were exacting criteria we figured we wouldn't have to deal with any potential spouses for awhile but it wasn't too many years after, not to mention many jokes about our tradition that young ladies began appearing in our home in the company of the oldest boys. The courting practices were thrown to the winds and we currently have two delightful daughters – in-law and are expecting our second and third grandchildren any day.

Most of the children are avid readers and even those that are not yet, have perused the Moomintroll series of books written by Tove Janssen (a Finnish author). Seth harbored a secret hope to be Snufkin and I often use Moominmamma as a password for various accounts. These books that I read as a child have become family favorites and I just recently purchased a set for my first grandson. Although he is not even one yet, I hope that he and his cousins and siblings will enjoy these books as much as my children did and pass this tradition on to yet another generation.

The Northumberland County Expo is another family favorite. It is such a small fair that almost anyone who enters nice vegetables can win a prize. This has launched a great deal of competition in the family as well as helped me get weeders for the garden. There are children out in the rows early in spring picking out the best red beet which no one can pick and eat until after the fair. David is on the hunt for the biggest pumpkins and watermelons that he can grow and everyone gets to enter something if they help at all.

Jerusha at the Northumberland County

These little traditions are a sort of super glue. To anyone outside the family, they are silly and meaningless but they help identify us as a part of the group. As children marry into the family they are initiated into our little traditions so they aren't clueless when we laugh about the Groak or wonder where the brownies went and they can join in. Perhaps all families need their set of small traditions to help bind them together and give a sense of identity. At least it works for us.

12.
Treasure Mountain

Seth sits in the barber chair first tonight. His floppy blond hair has finally gotten the best of him so tonight he requests a flat top. This is quite an unusual request for this particular sixteen year old. But Mark is up the challenge.

As he flings the purple cape around Seth's shoulders, the children begin talking about when they first moved to Dornsife, Our old red brick farm house sits at the foot of the Lower Mahanoy Mountain. It was a miracle that we even found this place out in the middle of nowhere but found it we did and it has proven a wonderful place to raise children. From the time we moved, the boys were bent on exploring every nook and cranny. There was a creek, a pine forest, a mountain behind the house and even a cave if you looked hard enough. One of the most exciting things we could do was climb to the top of the mountain, a lengthy hike for fairly small children.

One afternoon in late fall, Hannah Noah and David came to me and asked if they could go on a treasure hunt. My picture of a treasure hunt included a childish map drawn to represent various locations on the farm and a big X where the treasure was. This seemed reasonable and as the schoolwork was done, I assented and they ran off.

Now a treasure hunt requires a treasure, so the first order of business was to bury something. Hannah had a small box suitable for treasure which she contributed and they set off, not to hide in the barn or one of the pastures, but up the mountain. It was a beautiful day. Most of the leaves had fallen but the air was unusually warm for November. The leaves rustled and crackled underfoot and the sky was that peculiar bright fall blue. The only problem was the further up they went; the harder the trail was to see. Finally they reached a point where the trail ended and only rocks were left. "No problem" Hannah assured the others. "When we come back, we'll start down the trail right here and the top is just up there." as she pointed, they took new heart, scrambled to the top and buried the treasure under a large rock. Now all that was left to do was climb back down and draw a map for future treasure seekers.

It was late afternoon by now and the intrepid explorers had no clue that their mother was looking all over for them, thinking they were somewhere around the farm.

They hiked diligently down and down and it got darker and darker and somehow no one heard me calling and calling them. I was finally ready to call someone, anyone and report missing children when they showed up again. Naturally I went from being a slightly panic stricken mother asking God to help us find these three to being angry with them for being so thoughtless. How quickly we forget. Here God had brought them safely home and I don't recall ever saying "thank you" as I ran out to scold my errant children.

Our children have been AWOL other times too. When Elijah was under the age of two he would disappear and I would send everyone out searching the farm to figure out where he had gone when he slipped away from us. I finally figured out he would go up in his room, pull out the drawer that was under his bed and fall asleep in it. We also have a cliff on our land, small to be sure but when no one responded to the bell I ring for meals and emergencies and then an hour later my children showed up saying, "Oh Mom, we were only playing at the cliff."I wasn't very happy.

Misplaced children are one of those things that mothers wish upon their own children in a moment of frustration "Just wait until you have children".

Years later with only one or two remaining to get lost in such a fashion, I have learned to always assign a big kid to the smallest child and the amount of misplacing has diminished.

Since that first treasure hunt, there have been many more. Someone is always drawing maps and hiding candy for other siblings to find. It is an excellent babysitting tool if one plans ahead and there are several of my children who employ it regularly. Perhaps the best of these is David. Just last week, in an effort to get all his younger brothers and sisters outside so the house would be quieter, he made up clues and sent everyone off on a hunt through the spring house and the pine forest. They returned quite awhile later to discover that David had the winning clue and thus claimed to own the treasure even though he hid it in the first place. I secretly think there was never any treasure in the first place, but that has yet to be proven. While the small guys were empty handed David achieved his goal of some peaceful time alone and there will still be many treasure hunts to come because enthusiasm for them remains undimmed.

As our future cousin camps unfold we will probably have to have treasure hunts just to keep the tradition alive.

Average age of blue collar workers in Dornsife drops dramatically. Jedidiah, Ephraim and Moriah prepare to go to work.

13.
Labor Day

Typically the words Labor and Day used together conjure up thoughts of picnics, a respite from work, or perhaps the last fun day before school starts. Not so at our house.

We have found many new and exciting ways to define Labor Day. I personally celebrate sixteen labor days every year but the children call them birthdays. One of the Labor Days that the children think of first is the year our goat, Jingle, had twins on Labor Day and the children promptly named them Ding Dong and Belle. They still will say "Oh remember the Labor Day the goat was in labor and we all got to watch the kids being born" That was quite an exciting event for us all.

Probably less fondly they remember the Labor Day we decided to cement in the pond. We had quite a few cement blocks sitting around from various projects and our neighbor had a small cement mixer which he said we could borrow. A trip to Jones Hardware down the road produced sand and cement mix and we got up early to spend a day improving our pond.

In retrospect, we had no clue what we were getting into. The day stretched on and on, as we stacked cement blocks, mortared the cracks, added a drain pipe so we could clean the pond out every spring and there seemed no signs of the day ending. It stretched into about six weeks of mixing, mortaring, stomping and general stickiness. Ever try washing wet cement off small children's tennis shoes? We were getting desperate to finish the job when the State road crew passed by one fall day and told Mark they had too much cement left over from their project, "Would we have a place to dump it?"

Of course we did. right in the bottom of the pond. All the big children were pressed into service and we spent the rest of the day filling in all the places that had not gotten cement yet, smoothing it, and in general making a much nicer job than the little hand mixer was doing. This was an answer to prayer. Does God care about cement and ponds and children who think they are overworked? Yes He does. The pond is still in use. We have had to fix a crack or two every spring but instead of a mud hole, it is usable for many childish events and we can pull the plug out when necessary and power wash the algae down the drain. Not only that, but I go out every couple weeks and admire the handprints we left in the wet cement and think about how everyone has grown.

In other years more holidays than one have come to be known as labor days. We have gotten in the habit of purchasing old homes and renovating them, then reselling them. This has several advantages for our large family. When electrical work is slow, it provides side work, the boys who don't work for Mark but still need income for college tuition or car insurance have summer jobs and when we finally finish the project and sell it, we all benefit from a little extra income. In addition, the children are learning how to hang dry wall, simple electrical work, simple plumbing, how to paint walls and trim in a professional manner and many other skills which will stand them in good stead in the future when they have homes of their own. They are also learning how to stick at a job until it's finished and have the satisfaction and pride of seeing a job well done.

I have enjoyed watching a young boy see this huge project, a whole house that needs to be rewired, replumbed, redrywalled, sometimes needing a new roof or siding or possibly even some landscaping. At the beginning, there is excitement, followed by moans and groans as the project stretches across several months and finally new excitement when they see the end in sight, the house is done and sold and everyone can share in the benefits.

This past spring we bought two old houses, both of which were completely demolished inside. We are just beginning to work on them but several of the older children have asked to help. The girls often work as hard as the boys and they would rather work for us as a family than go out and work for strangers and they have learned the value of these projects. In turn, the younger children who are just beginning to learn some of these skills can see the example of their older siblings hard at work. It is not easy work. The kids come home filthy, tired and hungry and the farm chores still need done but it is rewarding and we are thankful for it. It has brought togetherness in adversity and, for some of my children, has had more educational value than their Math or English books and finally, it gives us a few more tales to tell when we sit around the kitchen table or in the barber chair.

Work crew: David, Jedidiah, Moriah, Ephraim, Noah and Benjamin

14.
A Clean House is a Relative Thing

Our Bathroom
Oh, thou necessity of every being
Always in need of dire cleaning

With wash scattered upon the floor
And muddy spots all over the door

There are five kids in that tub
Who all need a good scrub.

The sink needs a good scour
The kind given only with Mama Power

I think I'll leave out the toilet
In case, this poem, I might spoil it

And as for the rest, I'm sure you can guess
Our bathroom is always a terrible mess.
-Naomi Ilgenfritz (age 15)

A common misconception among people we meet is that I must be a really good housekeeper in order to have all these children. The assumption is that I have developed many effective systems for dealing with our messes. The reality is that I am just as ordinary as everyone else. I often have supper dishes in my sink till breakfast the next day because we are all tired by the end of the day. My bathroom is never as neat as I would like – not with eleven boys, and there are usually cobwebs on my ceiling. When company is coming on short notice, I sometimes collect all the clutter and throw it in my bedroom and lock the door. God's sense of humor came into play again one of those times as, looking for a bed to lie on while a headache passed, a guest went in and found my hidden clutter. I was surprised she could actually even find my bed.

Several years ago, I decided to give up on housekeeping. Please don't go into shock. I just couldn't balance my expectations about how a house should look with the reality of having sixteen children. I decided it was more important to have the children God was willing to give us than to stress out about the state of my home. Seth and I even came up with a little saying:" A clean house is a relative thing. When we see a relative, we clean it"

That still holds true. While we try to do some work on the place everyday, there is just too much else calling for our attention to sustain a long term program of spotlessness.

I can still remember as a girl of perhaps ten or eleven, reading *Christy* by Catherine Marshall. In one chapter, Firelight Spencer leaves off the unending work in her cabin to take the children out to the top of a mountain simply to enjoy a beautiful spring day. I wanted to enjoy life in the way she did. While it was hard and the drudgery sometimes seemed endless, she still lived life to the fullest and enjoyed it.

I do draw the line at cats and dogs in the house as creating more dirt than I want but lizards, tadpoles and other caged critters are allowed.

One year laundry was heavy on my mind almost continually so I wrote a little story about it and mailed it out for the family news that Christmas:

****

Dec 1998

A year to remember! I think mebbe it can best be summed up by this little tune wrote by Maw this year. If you've got a hankerin to sing, use the tune "Down in the Valley"

Down in the basement
Basement so low
Hang your head over
See the laundry pile grow.

You may ask why this particular song? Well, pull up yore rockin chair and put your feet up a spell whilst I tell you a story.

Oncet there was a mighty big crowd of children, went by name of Ilgenfritz. They lived with their maw and paw at the edge of a mountain. While most of them like to read or camp out in their big white tent, they most often found themselves doin such things as choppin wood, feedin animals or worst of all, helping reduce the emu population in the pasture.

Some of the big boys liked huntin and fishin. Some o the gals liked fishin right well too. The little guys mostly played a lot, inside or outside.

Well, one day their maw was down sortin through the wash and singin her song when David came a runnin in and said "Maw, Maw, Peaches done got out o her pen again."

Now Peaches was a cute little pig but she laked to get out now and then and David bein only five needed some help catchin her.

Seth, the oldest boy had got himself a passel o fine golden retrievers, but he called them guys "pig dogs." He left Rascal lose to round up Peaches. Peaches, she took off and headed straight up the mountain. Benjamin was a tryin' to head her off and didn't he go and fall in a big ol patch o poison ivy. Now Ben, he was mighty allergic so he come runnin in the house, took them clothes off, threw em in the wash and jumped in the shower. Josiah, meanwhile, thought he saw a shortcut through his heifer's pasture. He was arunnin so fast he tripped in his maw's big boots and he allus liked to wear and fell in… you guessed it. Well he needed a bath too.

Since the big boys was out o commission, Hannah and Naomi thought mebbe they bein girls could outthink a little ole pig. They saddled up Zaccheus, their donkey and lit out after the pig. Peaches, she were pretty smart, she circled around, ran thru the briars and neither the dogs nor the donkey could follow her in thar. Naomi tried to run on in but got herself full o them boogie lice, what sticks on yore clothes. She was too itchy, she had to go change and threw her clothes on down in the wash pile. Maw was still sortin out clothes down there.

Well, Elijah and Jedidiah weren't too big, but they crawled in the briar patch and scared that pig out. Peaches run and run. Rascal got her in sight again and next thing you know she run through the shallow end of the pond. Noah and Esther was out fishin. That pig were in such a hurry she run right into the back of Noah, he tripped on that slippery bank, grabbin at Esther to catch him as he went. They both fell in the mud and needed a bath. Now Maw was feedin their new baby brother, Moriah. Til she got to the bathroom to help all the little guys, the towels all needed washed too.

Whoo-ee, only Ephraim were left to catch a pig, everyone else bein in the shower or the tub (good thing this family had three showers) well, him bein only a year old and barely walkin, it didn't look good. He was a standin in the barn with a big ole apple in his hand. Peaches she loved apples and lo and behold if she didn't just follow him right on in her pen. Course til he give her the apple he was kinda dirty too, not being any taller than the pig. Well that was the end of Peaches' adventure. All that was left was for their Maw to wash all them dirty clothes.

****

Since then we have expanded to two washers and two dryers instead of just one.

Some of the dilemmas we have encountered and never solved include matching socks. We have tried every system ever invented. The closest thing we got to success was pinning all the socks together with diaper pins before they went into the wash. This didn't work well with the small children as they had trouble with the pins. Benjamin mastered the system the best. He pinned his socks, threw them in the wash, they all came out matched and when he put them on, he pinned the safety pin to his belt loop. He returned from a mission trip once and a mom who had gone along told me, "We always knew Ben's socks. They were pinned" No name tags for him.

When you consider that I will buy one or two bags of socks for each child (perhaps at Christmas time) and there are six pairs to a bag, you have anywhere from 96 to 192 pairs of socks floating around the house. The washer will eat at least a third of the pairs before the next gift giving occasion and then other halves disappear in such strange places as behind the toilet, in the dirt pile, under the front porch and other random places.

Mark used to keep his socks safe because they were bigger than everyone else's but he has had to resort to initialing them or writing numbers on them or even dying them different colors so the big boys can't claim they didn't know whose socks they were.

Silverware is another item that seems to go AWOL frequently. I can usually find the missing pieces outside where an amateur archeologist has used them for excavations but often they are not in such a state that I care to reuse them.

Then there are the dust kitties and cobwebs. I am beginning to think that each child has an allotment of such dirt that comes with him or her. It's not your house but how many kids you have that determines the amount of cobwebs. We have invested in several nifty cobweb sweeping implements through the years but cobwebs still seem to multiply faster than we can keep up with them.

When I was young, I thought the attic was the place to store cool things that my grandchildren would find in later years when I was gone and enjoy. Our attic, however, is simply the storage place for all the clutter I don't know what to do with and someday hope to sort out. When ever I gird up my loins for this task, some small child finds me up there and discovers that he or she is sentimentally attached to whatever box of clutter I am attempting to throw away.

We have a burn pile out behind the barn. When I collect enough stuff, I get one of the big boys to help me haul it out there and light it up before the little guys see it. I have to be careful who I ask or everything will slowly make its way back into the house when I am not looking, sort of like silt filling up the river bed.

So if you plan to pay me a visit, call at least 15 minutes ahead. That way I can at least collect all the clutter and throw it into my bedroom and lock the door until you leave.

15.

In Sickness and in Health

The girls are rarely recipients of Mark's barbering skills, however, rare occasions do require it and those occasions often involve catastrophe of some sort, such as small girls trying out their hairstyling skills with a scissors. The most impressive of these catastrophes was our encounter with a plague of lice.

Far be it from me to imply that all of life is a bed of roses here. We have disasters strike, both big and small. Some of them have been life changing and some merely inconveniences that taught us life lessons but our house is as normal as anyone else's.

I can now identify with the Egyptians when the plagues of lice came their way. One summer we caught lice from someone who visited us and stayed overnight. Rumor has it that he told the boys "look I have lice" and rubbed his head over them, completely unaware of the long term ramifications. The boys didn't bother to tell me this until several months later because they also thought he was just kidding. I heard about 2 weeks after he was here, that his mom had found a louse on him and done the treatment etc. We didn't see any on our kids and life went its merry way until several weeks later, Mark and I were visiting Seth and Seth's in laws were also there. Hannah called from home and said,

"Mom, on the way home from Church, I found lice on Ephraim's head."

She promptly sent everyone outside and wouldn't let them come back until we bought the proper shampoo. After a very late night of washing and combing and picking, we thought we had everything under control. Alas, it was not to be.

Lice treatment involves a non-complicated but extremely time consuming treatment program. Special shampoos must be purchased and applied, then all the hair carefully combed from the scalp to the ends. It took hours to get through the girls' long hair. The boys were easier, Mark gave them all a buzz and we could see any lice fairly easily. The girls have long lovely hair and Hannah, Naomi and Esther refused to part with theirs. Hosannah and Jerusha weren't given an option and spent their time in the barber chair just like the boys. Add to this the fact that all the sheets of the afflicted person have to be washed. Stuffed toys can be thrown out or bagged up and frozen for several weeks to kill any potential lice. Ten days later, the whole process has to be repeated to insure successful treatment and no one with lice is supposed to attend school. Now multiply this times thirteen children who still live at home.

We spent months wrestling with lice and hundreds of dollars on lice killing products. It wasn't until the next summer that I was sure we were free of all lice nits, etc. Some of my children were more embarrassed than others to have lice, but as a mom it certainly wasn't something I wanted spread around. We finally had to just laugh whenever more lice were found, keep everyone home from school (they didn't mind that part) and keep after them. I'm sure this was some sort of character developing effect on all of us or perhaps just preparation for those of my children who may end up on the mission field some day.

Still, nothing strikes fear into my heart quite so quickly as when someone comes home from school and says "there was a lice check in our class today."

One year we decided to rip the carpet out of our living room and turn it into part of the kitchen – one big dining/ cooking area. No sooner had we got all the old flooring ripped out than stomach flu struck. At the time we had eleven children and for the first time since I can remember, everyone got it simultaneously. There were people lying on sofas, chairs, beds, anywhere close to a bathroom. Then there were all the sheets to wash since small children have a great deal of trouble actually reaching the bathroom or even a near by basin in time. In addition, the week before, I had tripped and hit my jaw bone on the corner of a workbench in the basement. I could barely open my mouth. In the process of x-rays to make sure my jaw wasn't broken, I found out I was expecting a baby. So there I was throwing up from the flu or from baby nausea and I could barely open my mouth. Mark was trying to lay adhesive tiles in the kitchen and he was sick too. He would lay a few tiles, and then lie down on the floor till he felt better and then lay a few more tiles.

We made it through that episode and went twelve years without everyone getting sick all at the same time. This winter we decided to put in a new floor as we had worn the old one out. The boys were home from college and so I made a special meal of their favorite pork and sauerkraut. They ripped the old floor out and I cooked and we all sat down for a special meal. I wondered why so many of them said "Mom, I'm not very hungry tonight", until, in the middle of the night, seven kids were running to the bathroom. Before the week was out, we all had it. It will be many years before I ask for a new kitchen floor again.

Some of the more interesting adventures we have occur when Mark is gone. He is part of a group of men and boys known as Royal Rangers, similar to Boy Scouts. Several different years he has gone to training camps and he also attends the Frontier Camping Fellowship events with the older boys twice yearly. This gives ample opportunity for adversity to strike and allows time for me to exercise my ingenuity.

There are some years that stick in my memory more than others. The year Esther was a baby for example. We had seven children ages nine to one and Mark left to attend a National Training Camp for leaders. Before he left, we took our van to the garage because it needed some minor brake work.

Since this left me without a vehicle, we had arranged with Joyce, my mother-in-law to drive us to the garage which was about 45 minutes away. It rained the whole way there and back and as I pulled into the driveway, I stepped on the brakes – what brakes? The van slid the whole length of the driveway and was only stopped by sliding into the garage door. Rather flustered, I herded everyone into the house and made supper.

All went well until the next morning when two year old Noah somehow put his hand through the glass window of the back door leaving glass everywhere. Fortunately, there were no serious injuries and after applying band aids and masking tape to the appropriate places we decided to lie low for the day and try to avoid any catastrophes. We laid so low, that I decided rather than haul everyone to Church in a defective vehicle; we would just stay home and sleep in. I forgot to mention the sleep- in part to Benjamin who was eight at the time. Since Dad was gone, he decided to be helpful and found the baby walker which I had put away thinking Esther was too old for it. He got Esther out of her crib and put her in the walker. The only problem was the walker and Esther and all the children were on the second floor. Esther immediately fell down the stairs and hit the metal gate at the bottom which I had put there to keep her from going up and getting hurt. Once again, there were no serious injuries, just a shook up Mom and a baby with two black eyes. We did call a nurse, my mother – in –law who is an RN and there was no evidence of concussion. This was all three weeks before David decided to make his appearance. It's a wonder it didn't put me into labor.

Another year I can recall, we were living on the farm and had goats. I still am not sure why anyone would choose to have goats. We thought they were to eat our poison ivy but the goats never agreed to this arrangement. They also needed to be milked. This particular weekend the big boys went camping with Mark. Somehow I had to keep track of all the small children and keep them from getting hurt while milking two ornery goats.

I chose to make the goats wait until the kids went to bed, tied them in the barn and milked them while running up to the house every now and then to make sure no one had awakened. In the morning I got up very early before anyone else and got all the milking done before the children could get up and find disaster. That system worked for the two days the boys were gone but I have not milked since unless it was just to get acquainted with a new cow.

When Seth was a junior in high school he was invited to attend a one week forum for high school students interested in medicine. We all drove to Philadelphia together to drop him off but Mark had to work the day that Seth was finished. The rest of us got up at 6:00am, loaded all the children plus my visiting niece into the van and set off for an adventure in Philadelphia.

Perhaps I shouldn't have been so cheerful. It rained so hard on the turnpike that we could barely see the road but the Lord kept us on the right path and we made only one wrong turn. After spending six and a half hours in the van, we arrived home again still in one piece. The sun had come out and I sent all the little guys out to play to use up their excess energy. I had barely turned around when Elijah came back in; Ephraim had accidentally hit him in the head with a hoe. While I was contemplating if this needed stitches or not, Naomi came in. She and David were building a fort out of old lumber and she had hammered her finger. This event was followed by Mary (my thirteen year old niece) and Hannah going for a pony ride where a yellow jacket promptly stung Hannah on the lip. They abandoned the pony in favor of a quest for blackberries where Elijah, now recovered from the hoe incident, joined them. He was soon back in because a hornet stung him on the finger. I am sure the children wondered why I sent everyone to bed before 7:30 on a nice summer evening but some days you just quit and start over and think of Anne Shirley saying "Every day is fresh with no mistakes in it".

The Golden Road of Youth

Emmanuel and some of his friends

16.

Going To the Dogs

A good topic of supper time conversation is often our pets and the dogs we have are no exception. Usually these tales have some relationship to our small dog breeding operation and our more interesting customers.

Somewhere in Seth's early life he decided he would like to be a physician of some sort. Not too long after that, he developed a vision for breeding golden retrievers in order to help raise college funds.

His first retriever, "Jules" named after Jules Verne, met an untimely end after tangling with a rabid raccoon. Shortly after that he acquired two females, Rusty and Candy and another male named Rascal. His dog breeding career was well launched and then Benjamin got in the game with the purchase of another female, Dandy.

Somehow, my mothering talents were transmogrified from a mom who tenderly bathed and diapered babies to a woman who was willing to bathe twelve five- week old puppies in her kitchen sink. I considered charging a fee for my services except that I couldn't foot Seth's college bills either. Thus I figured he might as well just keep all his money.

Seth and Benjamin, were quite the entrepreneurs, and through their efforts, they built a nice new dog kennel, Seth bought his first car, they paid their dog food and vet bills and then began saving.

Since Seth went on to earn enough scholarships to fund his undergraduate studies, some of the puppy money went on to help Josiah attend LeTourneau University and work towards his mechanical engineering degree.

As the boys went off to school the job of selling pups fell more and more on my lap.

Most of the time I enjoy meeting new people but puppy marketing has its unexpected side. You never know what kind of people you will be meeting when you make an appointment. Anyone from someone who thinks they can't buy a puppy because it wasn't born in a house but a nice heated kennel to someone who wants two big hairy retrievers to sleep in bed with them.

Selling puppies has taught me humility. My small children's favorite occupation is showing off to potential customers. I have learned that when a potential buyer has an appointment, I must assign a big child to keep all the small guys in the house watching a video with the door shut to avoid an embarrassing show. The other day I forgot my usual precautions and several children found themselves hanging (literally) on my long clothesline with a piece of toy that worked as a zip line, while the couple who came to pick out a dog watched in interested and perhaps unbelieving silence.

The same couple wanted to see Alice, my mother dog. I called and called and she finally showed up with a rotten piece of a snapping turtle's head in her mouth. The real me would have smacked her until she dropped it and then shoveled it up and burned it. The me that is a sales person was polite and said, "Alice, whatever are you eating? Drop that right now"

Of course she didn't but just stood and chewed it up as we watched. She smelled of rot from several feet away. Then the visiting wife bent over, took Alice's head between her hands and crooned into her face,"Nice girlie, aren't you a nice baby", while Alice's maggot breath panted out at her. I felt a little sick but they bought a puppy so who was I to argue.

Then there was the year when my best mama dog had her puppies and several of them died. After a vet autopsy, we found out we had had an undesirable bug and so had to completely disinfect and quarantine our kennel for a while. It was winter so we put our pups in the basement with their mama. In the meantime, my grandmother died and Mark and I flew out to Minnesota for the funeral. The children, being unused to a dog in the house and the dog being unused to reporting her need to visit the outdoors, we came home to a completely ruined living room carpet, and several disgusted children. After replacing the carpet we sent the dogs back outside to their now clean kennel. When a couple came to look at puppies shortly after that, one of the children was quick to point out, "Oh, we had a lot more but some got sick and died"

True information, but not exactly how I would have expressed it to a customer.

On the other hand, we have had customers bring baskets of goodies to ease the pain of a puppy leaving our home (I think only Emmanuel has felt any real pain over leaving, but who argues with bringers of candy?) and our latest customer very generously brought us gum and toothbrushes and cold remedies enough to last for years. They were from his factory and were simply items that for one reason or another couldn't be sold but they so enjoyed bringing them to our kids.

I shared them with our married children and sent some of the items to Africa with the children's aunt and uncle for their use, so lots of people benefited from this couple's generosity.

As much as I am an animal lover, I have always told the children," You guys bring enough dirt into the house without animals coming in here."

And so as often as I get requests for my cute fuzzy dogs to come live indoors with us, I have always refused them. Perhaps when I am old I shall recant and when the great grandchildren come to visit me, there will be dogs and cats and a parakeet in my house and my children will say,"How come you never let us do that?"

To which I will cheerfully reply," It's a woman's prerogative to change her mind." and offer to send a pet home with whatever child asked the question.

Esther and Emmanuel enjoying a fall day

17.
The Things We Do For Love

I can distinctly remember a time in my life, around age 14 when I said I would never marry a farmer. So, I didn't. I married a college boy who majored in Religious Education. Little did I know that he would transform into an electrician and then ever so gradually, into a farm boy.

As we moved from house to house, each time we added a little more country. Our first apartment we only owned chickens, three Canadian geese and a dog. Our next move eliminated all the animals but then they began to multiply again. Living in York City, Pennsylvania, we had six chickens in the backyard and any number of rabbits in the basement. Selling that property and moving out to five acres on the edge of town, we gained more chickens, more rabbits, a dog again and eventually ten emus. When the Township powers-that-be decided to crack down on the fact that we were zoned residential, even though surrounded by cornfields, we bought the small farm we currently live on.

Thus I became married to a farmer and have enjoyed most of the farming life. There are a few events along the way though, that have caused me some raised eyebrows. One that comes to mind is related to our enjoyment of pork. Our family owned two big sows that we decided to breed instead of butcher. We thought we would raise piglets instead and get more pork for our investment.

The first pig produced eleven piglets quite efficiently all by herself. The second sow kept getting bigger and bigger. One day I had gone grocery shopping and returned to find Mark, my husband down in the pig pen with the second mama. He saw me drive in and yelled at me, "Hurry up and change clothes, I need you down here"

Not sure of the problem, I rushed off to change and then down the path to the pig pen.

"This pig's in labor and she can't deliver "he announced. "You're going to have do help her out because my arm is too big."

"ME, I'm just a mom, not a midwife. Besides, how would I know what to do?"

Apparently he had already thought of that because our cousin Melissa used to work for a pig farmer delivering piglets and Mark had already called her for advice.

"All you have to do" I was informed, "is grease your arm with Vaseline and reach up inside the pig and get the first baby out to get things started"

Imagine a large sow weighing several hundred pounds and in labor with my arm inside of her. I had visions of writing another James Herriot book even as I dutifully greased my arm. Sure enough, there was a baby in there but he didn't want to come out. Every time the pig had a contraction, that little guy would scoot backwards instead of forwards. Then there was the fact that he was so slippery. It was hard to get a grip on those little legs. Eventually I got him out. Thinking that was it, I prepared to clean up. It was not to be though. The other piglets were equally stubborn and refused to be born of their own free will. Finally I successfully delivered nine piglets, all healthy and noisy and we thought all was over. Imagine our surprise the next morning when we went to check on Mrs. Pig and found two additional piglets that had shown up in the night. They were healthy too and we spent a lot of hours enjoying our piglets until they grew big enough to escape from any pen ever designed.

We would come home from an errand and find a herd of pigs under the apple trees or rooting in the garden or visiting our neighbors and had to reinforce all our fencing which was only designed for large pigs, not small slippery babies.

Another event that strikes me funny now, though not at the time, occurred even before the pig episode.

Living on a small farm as we do, it was inevitable that our family would have to get farm animals. That thought being established, the obvious choice was a cow. Since we have many mouths to feed - twelve at the time, a nice beef variety seemed in order.

"Remember Elsie", my son Benjamin asked, just the other day.

How could Elsie be forgotten? Among the various cows and steers we have had, she is notable, not only because she was our first, but because she had decided ideas of where home was.

Elsie was a half grown red and white Hereford when we purchased her and she had obviously never been someone's pet. This didn't matter to us though, because we knew that she was destined for a short life with a future as ground beef and sirloin steak and we certainly did not want the children getting attached to her.

Being spontaneous in our purchases, we put the cart before the horse and had no fenced- in pasture for cattle. My husband figured that one heifer barely qualified as needing pasture so she sported a chain collar and a bell and we tied her every day in a new spot so she could chew down the vegetation and add to her girth.

This system worked fairly well for a while. Since they were the oldest sons, Seth and Benjamin would drag her out in the morning or, depending on her mood, she would drag them or Mark, my husband would attach her long chain to the tractor and help her along to the new grazing spot while the boys followed with a large bucket of water.

One morning Elsie must have decided that the grass was greener elsewhere. Somehow she broke her chain and ran off. We hadn't had her very long yet and so we were afraid she wouldn't know her way home. Not only that, but various neighbors kept calling and saying, "Your cow is in my flower bed." or

"Hey, I just saw your cow run past here. Is she dangerous?"

A week went by with Elsie sightings every day but no one could catch her. We tried sneaking up behind her until the children were convinced that she had some sort of radar system. Then we tried waiting until nightfall and creeping close but she was wary of any unusual noises and children under the age of twelve are not very quiet sneaking through the brush. Not only that, but she always chose a patch of poison ivy to lie in and it is difficult to get someone to sneak through poison ivy after they have tried it once. She would return at night to get water from our stream, we would hear her bell jingling and jangling and mount a capture attempt, but no one could get close enough to grab her collar.

Then, as in many other significant moments in our family history, Mark had to go out of town leaving me about seven months pregnant and with all ten of the children to look after. A car stopped in our driveway.

"Do you own a big red and white cow?" the stranger asked.

"Who wants to know?" was my response.

"Well I just saw one headed towards the post office and someone said it could be yours".

"Thanks", I said, relieved that she hadn't destroyed anyone's prize winning begonias.

In record time, I loaded all the children into the van and set off towards the post office. Sure enough, there was Elsie, walking placidly along the highway. I pulled off the road, jumped out and got her to turn around and head back towards our house. Then I ran back to the van as fast as my pregnant belly would allow, hoping all the while that the kids wouldn't try to drive off on their own or wrestle inside and put the car into neutral by accident. I jumped in and followed her towards our house. It's not easy to herd a cow in a fifteen passenger van. Every time she showed signs of heading back towards the post office, we pulled off, got out of the car and shooed her back the right way. While fervently hoping no one would look out their windows and see a pregnant woman running down the road after a cow, I was also secretly hoping I could capture her and impress Mark with my animal handling skills.

Much to my disappointment, as soon as we came in sight of our land, she veered off into the brush and disappeared. Finally we called a fellow who owned a tranquilizer gun, located her in an evening when she was preparing to sleep and shot her with a tranquilizer dart after which we returned her to her chain, now made stronger, and in a fit of pique, changed her name to T-bone.

I have come to the conclusion that I love being a farmer's wife and I recommend country living to all my city friends even as they shake their heads at me, for where else could I have gone to have such an interesting and exciting life.

Reaping the potato harvest

18.
Been There, Done That

When I was expecting Benjamin, our second child, we went to a cabin for a short vacation with some friends of ours. I was bemoaning the fact that Mark didn't help get Seth ready for church on Sundays. My friend Nancy reassured me that one or two children are normal for Mom to handle and by the time we had our third baby, Mark would chip in and help get everyone ready. Now that we have sixteen, I do have help on many Sundays but it is not my husband, it is usually my teenage daughters.

This has bugged me off and on for years until just recently, I was reading a magazine and another wife was expressing what I thought I alone was dealing with. She had to get up and get the kids ready and her husband slept in. Reading that, I said to myself "This is me."

By the time I get to church I am often frustrated, I'm distracted and I could just as easily leave everyone and go sit in the car. God was speaking to me through someone else's testimony. After 25 years of getting small children ready for church, I felt I was finally on the verge of finding an answer. My acts of obedience and sacrifice to get everyone ready for church don't need to end in frustration. They can be an act of worship in and of themselves and my sacrifice of obedience to God.

This thought led me to begin to reflect on many other areas of my life as a mother and how I relate to Mark and my children. When I'm really frustrated with the progress of life and my blessings are overwhelming me, I remind myself of the verse in Matthew 18:5 "And whoever receives and accepts and welcomes one little child like this for My sake and in My name receives and accepts and welcomes Me." (Amplified version) or the verse in Matthew 10:42, where it says,"And if anyone gives even a cup of cold water to one of these little ones…I tell you the truth, he will certainly not lose his reward." Some nights when I have been asked by four or five children for a drink of water, I have to stop and think of this verse. A cup of water is such a small act of service but I would certainly jump up and get it if Jesus sat here and asked me. Why not for one of the children He has given me.

Every one of the children in my house, I am to treat as if he or she was Christ. This is slowly changing some of the ways I chose to do things. Would I yell at Jesus if He were sitting at my table and accidentally spilled the milk? Of course not, but my initial reaction to my children is to yell. These aren't even things I've never heard before. God has just chosen to remind me of them again and as I am a slow learner at times, He will probably have to remind me of them many more times before my job here is finished.

Titus chapter two is often quoted as a passage to encourage us either as older women to be an example and helper to younger wives or, when I was younger, to seek for an older woman who could be of help and teach me. While I do have many friends who are older women and they have been wonderful teachers for the most part, I do regret never having found someone who had a large houseful of children, had learned how to deal with all the issues that arise just from volume, and then could pass this information on to me. I'm so thankful that God is a faithful teacher and I am learning as I go. I certainly do not have all the answers. My newest lessons involve how to let go of young married children and encourage them to make their own family. This will probably take many years to learn since only two of our children are married but I am trying to be open to how God wants me to make this transition.

Ecclesiastes, chapter 3 verse 1 reminds me," To everything there is a season, and a time for every matter or purpose under heaven:

This season that I am entering will be just as challenging as the one filled with preschoolers or the one right after my first miscarriage when we wondered if God would ever give us children. I can look back at that season and laugh now that we have sixteen children but we cannot see the future, we can only be faithful in what God has shown us right now to do. Today it's laundry and dishes and wiping small behinds. Tomorrow it may be moving to another country and sharing the gospel with unreached peoples but I can't see tomorrow yet.

I met a family the other day who had four children aged five and under and they were expecting a baby. I thought to myself, this was me 20 years ago. I have been there and done that. When I went home, I begin to think about what I could do to encourage this mom that she can make it. She is at a hard time in life with so many little ones but the rewards she has not even seen yet. I' m just beginning to see some of the rewards from this work and perhaps I will never know the whole picture but my prayer is continually that God can use me to be an example to my children of a godly, faithful wife and mother and if I can encourage other moms that He would use me to encourage other moms. I may have eleven daughters in law eventually. I want God to use me in their lives, not say "This is how to do it!" as if I am some expert, but just to encourage them to seek Him who can show them how it should work in their families.

One thing I have learned is not to compare our family with anyone else's. This first came to me through home schooling. When Seth and Benjamin were ready for kindergarten, we enrolled them in the local Christian school. I had never even heard of home schooling. Several years later, we began to get some exposure to what we thought was a radical change in life but by the time we were expecting our seventh child, we decided to die in and give it a try. I went from one side of the pendulum – Christian school for Christian families- to the other side – surely Christians would only chose to home school.

After several years and four babies later, I had home school burnout. Or so I thought. We decided to investigate Christian schools again. At that point we enrolled some of the children and kept our two older ones home to finish out the year. The next fall we enrolled everyone but since then, there have been years where everyone was home and years where they were all in school and years where we did both.

So what did all this pendulum swinging teach me? Mark and I need to know what is best for our family. Some kids need more time at home, sometimes God wants them in a school setting, but the bottom line is – Seek God for His will for your family. Do not compare how you do things with someone else because what works for them may not work for you. You have different personalities then any other family. I don't mean don't ask someone's advice. We ask lots of advice and try to find out what works for other families but then we bring that information home and weigh it against what we already know works for us and what we sense God wants us to do in any particular situation.

Just for example, the year we had eight children they were ages nine and under and I had just begun reading a mom –friendly magazine. In one issue, the editor interviewed a woman who had raised eight children and she said she never went to bed with her kitchen dirty. Even if she had to stay up until two or three in the morning after a big gathering, she always got up to a clean kitchen. I was sure this was the answer to my life's chaos but found it did not work for us. As soon as I had some routine, I was pregnant and sick again. I spent several years feeling guilty because I wasn't the ideal mom I wanted to be, but that plan simply didn't work for our family. So now, I often go to bed with dishes still in my sink. My house is not spotless, but we are all less stressed than if I was always hung up on my clean house.

When I am tempted to compare my life with others and feel guilty because I am not doing all the great things with my family that others do with theirs, I go back again to the Bible. Philippians 1:6 reminds me "And I am convinced and sure of this very thing, that He who began a good work in you will continue until the day of Jesus Christ." (Amplified) or Psalm 138:8 which states, The Lord will perfect that which concerns; Your mercy and loving-kindness. O Lord, endure forever…"

Honestly, If I couldn't retreat to my room and open the Bible, I don't know that I would make it as a Mom but I think this is how God wants me, dependent upon Him and not myself.

Let me leave with you a few final verses. Deuteronomy 4:7 which tells me:" For what great nation is there who has a god so near to them as the Lord our God is to us in all things for which we call upon Him." Or Psalm 139:5:"You have beset me and shut me in – behind and before and You have laid Your hand upon me." And Job 23:10 "But He knows the way that I take (He has concern for it, appreciates, and pays attention to it). When He has tried me, I shall come forth as refined gold. God has a lot of refining left on me but I am so glad He has concern for me and is willing to even bother with the refining process.

Celebrating National Pretzel Day with homemade soft pretzels:clockwise from left – Moriah, Jedidiah, David, Ephraim, Hannah, Esther, Elijah, Benjamin, Jerusha, Hosannah, and Noah with Mark and Miriam in the back

19.
The Rest of the Night

When I was a little girl, we always ate breakfast together around the table. My Dad would read the Bible and when he prayed he always said "Thank You for the rest of the night"

Being small, I thought sometimes he meant maybe the night wasn't over yet and there was more to come. Now that I am older I have come to see these words in a different light. When you are without sleep some or most of the night for over 25 years you become very thankful for the rest you do get at night.

How has this state of affairs come about? It started with Seth. When he was born, Mark and I didn't know very much about babies. This dilemma seems to affect most first born children. He would cry and I would get up and attempt to figure out what his problem was. Eventually he learned to sleep all night and then Benjamin came along. Each year the learning process was repeated with a new baby. Start with little sleep, gradually get more as you and baby adjust to each other and then, just when the current model was sleeping all night, another pregnancy. First you can't sleep right because you are shaped like a watermelon and then the new baby starts the process over.

One would think that after sixteen children, we would have figured the system out and perfected it. We thought so too. Stephen started right in sleeping in bed with us, mostly because I was too tired to get up all the time with him. Then he was such a delicious fat little guy that we just enjoyed spending time, either sleeping or waking with him. And now, as I try to convince him that he can sleep with his bigger brothers, he is trying equally hard to convince me that he should stay in our bed.

Other things will rob your sleep too. For Seth, it has been a few babysitting experiences. One night Mark and I went away, leaving him in charge. He was always very conscientious about the children but on this particular occasion, everyone was tucked in bed and so he went up to his room to read. He heard a funny noise from the little boy's room but by the time, he got over there, he heard the front door open and shut. As he ran down the stairs, he might have reflected that Jedidiah was a consummate sleepwalker, but when he ran outside he heard a splash in the pond. Fortunately, our pond is only about a foot deep, for there was Jedidiah, still asleep, in the pond. Seth brought him back up and returned him to bed and then told us about it when we got home while poor Jedidiah had no recollection of the event the next morning. After that I wondered how many years of Seth's life Jedidiah had just erased and I was careful to lock our doors for several years, not to keep the bad guys out, but to keep the sleepwalkers in.

When Naomi was two, she would frequently wake up screaming in the night. I would go over to see her and find her asleep but screaming. Once we got her quieted down, she would go back to sleep but it is sometimes difficult for me to return to sleep after being startled awake by a piercing shriek.

Of course, there are the normal nights where a child is sick and so I stay up with him or her. Some of our children are very good at catching croup which requires some nighttime nursing and there are those who wake up because they are afraid of the dark or can't find the bathroom in the night. The years when everyone catches the flu at once contribute to sleepless nights as well.

Then there is a snoring issue in our house. I think Hannah started it. When she was small she had what a friendly nurse called "kissing tonsils". We could hear her snoring from quite a few rooms away. Removing the tonsils improved her greatly but the snoring moved on to other people. I hate to name names, but there are nights I cannot sleep for the snoring in my own bedroom. I have found that if I can get to sleep first, I may not hear it until some child wakes me up needing something and I have to try to get back to sleep. I cannot figure out how Mark can sleep through all the events that have happened in the middle of the night down through the years but he will often get up in the morning and say, "Well did you have a good night's sleep" and when I reply to the contrary he cannot believe it. He never heard a thing.

Studies have shown the importance of a good night's sleep to general health and well being. I even read one that detailed how many years of life a person lost for each month of interrupted, restless or complete absence of sleep. Since I am planning to live to be at least 100, I can only conclude that perhaps moms are a special breed and don't require as much sleep as all the rest of the world.

I wonder how much sleep a grandmother needs.

Josiah telling a tall tale

20.
On Reweaving the Tapestry

Parenting, in our home started normally enough. We were young and in love and had a beautiful baby boy. He threw cheerios and smashed carrots on the floor and we thought it was cute. His every new discovery delighted us and left us breathless, wondering what would be next. What was next was fifteen more children and they followed each other in rapid succession. The term close family is an understatement at our house.

I look at our family as a tapestry. Every member is a different color and texture of thread. Our interactions with each other produce the picture. As we added children to our family, the picture became more detailed and complicated. Then the children were old enough to begin leaving and some of the threads got tangled.

As we all know, parenting doesn't come with a manual and this end of it appears to be just as hard to figure out as the other. However, after watching five of my children leave home and anticipating another one heading off to college next year, I have noticed some trends among the children left behind. As life moves along I am trying to change and adapt and help the children through that same process.

I had to recognize that the kids left at home were feeling a sense of loss. When our oldest son Seth first left home, college was only an hour and a half away, but our 12th child, Moriah was only three and he had always been Seth's close buddy. He spent weeks in tears if I so much as went out of the room and to go into the bathroom was to invite a child to lay himself outside the door wailing till I came out. A peaceful soak in the tub was no longer an option till the weekends Seth came home. Moriah did eventually outgrow this but it threw a curve into life because I had never expected it.

We had to start training our children to work even when they weren't ready to do the job completely. When the first three had respectively gone off to college, become a homeowner and entered medical school, we realized that some of the others would have to step up to the plate and handle jobs my oldest three had always done. Oops, I never got around to training them. Suddenly younger kids had to learn how to roto-till the garden, how to chainsaw to fill our wood furnace for the winter, and how to milk the cow, which was always the domain of the oldest.

I certainly don't want to start doing jobs that I already gave up just because some of my older ones have gone. Time enough for that when my last child leaves home. There are other children old enough to help now.

We had a barn raising this fall. Nine of the boys helped and it was a wonderful bonding time with some of the younger boys who hadn't helped with such jobs before. Even the boys who had left home came to help and we enjoyed them as adults and friends now, not as little children who needed everything done for them. Sure we will miss having all of them here for every holiday but at the same time, we can celebrate seeing them become what God intended them to be and the younger ones can anticipate what they may decide to do when they are ready to leave home.

We have to remember to do fun things with those still home. No one has died. Sometimes we have trouble planning vacations because "everyone isn't home". Even holidays hear the refrain" We never did it this way when Ben was here." or "Can't we wait till everyone is home." No we can't wait. Our home life takes place with those children still at home and it is just as important even if a few have grown up and gone away. The old traditions we started when the first kids were little keep a common thread through the changes.

I also had to realize that while meeting one's future spouse was exciting for my child, another of my children is likely to be jealous. When Seth started courting Lindsay, our oldest daughter Hannah had a hard time adjusting. She and Seth had always been close friends and while she liked Lindsay as a girl friend, she wasn't ready to give her place with Seth over to someone outside the family.

We spent quite a bit of time with Hannah working through all these new feelings. It helped just to realize that it was a normal part of her growing up process and now that the marriage is almost 2 years old, Hannah and Seth have a great relationship that includes Lindsay and the arrival of a baby making Hannah an aunt. At the same time, Hannah has acquired a serious boyfriend and I am seeing some of those same jealous traits in one of her younger brothers so the process will have to be repeated.

Every child that leaves the house leaves a different sort of hole in the family fabric. This requires different threads to patch and changes the picture in the tapestry. Personally, I hate change and so do a lot of my children. But no matter how I feel, life is full of change and so after fighting it for almost 50 years, I have decided to embrace it and try to teach my children to do the same. Surprisingly enough, our house still has 11 children home but it seems I have more free time and I can be creative in ways I couldn't when all of life was about dishes and diapers.

I don't resent the dishes and diapers time, as it changed and grew me in many ways, but there are new horizons now. I'd like to take piano lessons, or learn a new language or read a lot of books or travel around the country visiting all my children's new families.

My 20 year old daughter, said, "It's not an empty nest, Mom, it's a new adventure. She calls it the "final frontier."

Today I hold my one year old in my arms and feel his fat sticky hands pat my face and this time I realize the time is going to fly past. By the time he is ready to leave home, the whole picture will have been rewoven but with God's grace, we will all be able to celebrate the changes and see how they have woven together to make a work of art.

Celebrating life

21.
"If at First You Don't Fricassee..."

There are so many things we have yet to learn. Many people assume that just because we have sixteen children, we are parenting experts. It just ain't true. Every child is different and so each one teaches us new things. I heard a speaker –who had ten children- say once that every child God gave her taught her another character quality. At the time I only had seven children but as time went on and more and more were added to us, I began to wonder exactly how deficient my character was.

Well, somewhere in the middle is the truth. These children are here because God has a plan for their lives but in the midst of that, each of their lives touching mine does develop something new in me that was not there before. Please don't panic and think that if God chooses to bless you with a crowd, it is because you are lacking somehow.

In home schooling, in teaching how to keep a house, in cooking, in every area, if what I tried doesn't work, I try some other way. Sometimes what I tried works for two children and then the next one to come along is designed so differently that a new plan is called for. No matter how hard I have fought it, I have learned to be flexible.

Seth was the model first child. Well, yes he was fussy, but that was because I was fairly ignorant of infants and their needs. Still, he survived and did everything pretty much when the doctor said babies should hit these milestones. He crawled on time, sat up on time, walked on time, and on and on. Then we had Ben. He was a horse of a different color. Looking back, I can see it was just his different personality, as Benjamin is not a go–getter but is much more laid back. He didn't do anything when he was supposed to. He didn't even bother to walk until he was almost eighteen months old. I was a little concerned that something was wrong with him but I learned pretty quickly; don't compare your children to each other. They are all different.

When Esther was a baby, she fussed and bawled and cried and had to be with someone day and night. Now I can see Esther is the social butterfly of the family and she needed constant interaction with people. The more people the better, in direct contrast to David who is still convinced that he will grow up to be a hermit.

Potty training was another time of learning as you go. When Seth was eighteen months or so, well-meaning but unnamed individuals suggested tactfully that he really should be potty trained. Silly me, I listened and spent hours of my time getting frustrated at my lack of success, not to mention the extra laundry. With Benjamin, I started a little later but still was frustrated. When Josiah came along, I said, "Forget it."

The day before he turned three, he came to me and said, "Mommy, I'm not wearing these diapers anymore."

And that was that. No muss, no fuss. How easy can it be? I have reached the conclusion that no one ever went to college who wasn't potty trained.

I am not against advice, but well meaning friends and relatives can be overwhelming. As parents, we should know our families' needs best. Gather all the advice, sift it out, use the good ideas and get rid of the stuff that will not work for you.

Home schooling was another of those "learn as you go" times. My oldest sister sent me a book about home schooling and introduced me to this radical concept. However, I was pretty sure this new idea wouldn't work and we put the children in a Christian school when they were old enough. Then some good friends invited us to attend a local home school convention. We were hooked. Home schooling was the best way. Surely if you were a Christian, you would home school your children. Over the protests and concerns of our family, we pulled Seth and Ben out of school to try it out for a semester. The following year we moved and home schooled everyone for a few years. Then when our twelfth baby was on the way I got home school burnout or maybe preschooler burnout and we once again sought out a Christian school for the children. We have been at both ends of the pendulum and finally swung down to the middle (does this mean we have stopped?) Every year we evaluate where the children are scholastically y and socially, we ask the kids to pray about it and together we decide who will be where. Some years everyone is in Christian School. Some years they are all home. Some years we do both with some at the Christian school and some I home school

As often as I warn people not to put me on a pedestal, I think they do anyway. Perhaps just the idea that we have so many children is grounds for this, but we are so ordinary. When we meet new friends they often comment on how we must do things so well or be so patient and on and on and every now and then I must just tell some tales to prove them wrong.

One year when we had eight children, I took all the ones who were too small to attend school to see their big brothers in a Christmas play at school. I was quite particular to dress everyone up in their best so no one would think we couldn't look nice since we had so many kids (this is one misconception in my head but I take pains to prove it wrong). I had all the girls in cute matching Christmas dresses and had even made myself a matching maternity dress for I was expecting again. I was also rather proud of the fact that I had finally potty trained Naomi. She was sitting on my lap in her cute little frilly underwear that I let her wear and we were all engrossed in the play when suddenly, my lap was flooded. As my face turned red, I realized I was trapped. Mark hadn't come along so if I got up and left with Naomi, all the other little children would reveal their true behavior patterns while I was out changing her and then too, I was soaked and didn't bring a spare dress along in my diaper bag. Finally I just sat stiffly through the rest of the program with Naomi on my lap and didn't visit with anyone on our way out the door. I was hoping someone might think my water broke instead of suspecting that I was soaked with urine but once again I had to just forget my pride and realize perhaps my potty training methods weren't fool proof. We all made it home and I may be the only one who even remembers that night unless there are acquaintances of mine out there somewhere still wondering why I was so unfriendly one winter evening.

Publicity comes our way every now and then. One year we had a call from a local newspaper asking if they could do a story on our family. At first we turned them down, but on further reflection we decided to go ahead and let the paper run a story. They sent a photographer and a very nice young lady out to interview us. She asked everyone questions and spent a good part of the day with us. The story ran on the front cover of our local paper on Mother's Day and the headline proclaimed in big bold letters "I'm Never Tired and I'm Never Bored".

I got more response from that headline that I ever dreamed possible especially since it was a misquote and I actually said," I'm never lonely and I'm never bored"

I sent a copy of the article to my mother without explanation and she called up and accused me of being in denial. While the reporter called me up to apologize for the mistake, she never printed a correction and, now that almost nine years have passed, every now and then I'll run into someone who says

"Oh, are you that lady in the paper who is never tired?"

About two weeks after that, I was out in the car and got pulled over by a policeman. I was pretty sure I hadn't been speeding but as he scolded me for having my car out of inspection I was envisioning a new headline <u>Mother of 13 Cited For Improperly Securing Two Year Old in Car Seat.</u> That would surely make me sound like the Mother of the Year. Mark had our van so I had five pre- schoolers in a car designed for 4 passengers and according to the car seat law; some of them were illegally buckled in. I wouldn't have even gone out, but David and Noah's first grade class was having a Mother's Lunch which all good mothers must attend. So, while doing my duty I was "forced' to violate the law. Well, such is life. I suppose most mothers don't have five preschoolers to take with them to a first grade luncheon.

I have finally reached the conclusion that there is no possible way I can please all the child rearing experts I meet. A book I read years ago (Caddie Woodlawn) had the phrase in it "If at first you don't fricassee, fry, fry a hen"

That has stuck with me all my life and applies to parenting as well. If it doesn't work, try again, try another method but stick at it. Therefore, while I do ask advice when perplexed and have read my share of parenting books, only God can be the ultimate authority and I have only to answer to Him for the task He has given me. When my time on earth is up, I sincerely hope I will be remembered as a godly woman and one who put her family first.

Emmanuel and Jerusha practicing their singing skills while Hosannah and Ephraim attempt a four hand piano piece.

22.
Who Is Building The Cathedral?

I'm going to start writing on surveys and applications and IRS forms that I am a construction worker. I didn't start out this way. I was planning to be a single lady missionary, but now, somehow, I have been transformed into a builder. For the last 25 years Mark and I have been working hard on building. So, what exactly are we building? We are helping to build the church. Some of these ideas are recent thoughts and some we have been pondering for years. Neither Mark nor I feel that we have "arrived" in any way. We are working and learning as we go but they are thoughts and ideas we are sharing with our children as they grow up and start their own families.

Last year, as part of our devotions, we started studying the shorter catechism. The first question is: What is the primary purpose of man? And the answer: To glorify God and enjoy Him forever.

God has given us sixteen children and our full time job right now is to pass on to them the truths we know about the Kingdom of God and to teach them that the plan God has for their life is the best way they can glorify Him as well as enjoy Him. And God does have a plan for each one that He has given us.

Deut: 6: 4-9: says, "Hear, O Israel! The Lord is our God, the Lord is one! You shall love the Lord your God with all your heart and with all your soul and with all your might. These words which I am commanding you today, shall be on your heart. You shall teach them diligently to your sons and shall talk of them when you sit in your house and when you walk by the way and when you lie down and when you rise up. You shall bind them

117

as a sign on your hand and they shall be as frontals on your forehead. You shall write them on the doorposts of your house and on your gates." This is our foundation that we are building upon.

I have been doing a little research this spring: A 2002 survey conducted by the Southern Baptist Council on Family Life found that "88% of the children in evangelical homes leave the Church by age 18" This is a scary thought, but also has helped me focus on my job of passing my faith to the next generation.

Deut. 11:18-21 almost repeats the passage in Deut: 6, mentioned above. "Therefore you shall lay up these words of mine in your heart and in your soul, and bind them as a sign on your hand, and they shall be as frontlets between your eyes. You shall teach them to your children, speaking of them when you sit in your house, when you walk by the way, when you lie down, and when you rise up. And you shall write them on the doorposts of your house and on your gates, that your days and the days of your children may be multiplied in the land of which the Lord swore to your fathers to give them, like the days of heaven above the earth."

I don't know about you, but I want the days of my children to be multiplied! Matt: 28; 19, the passage we like to call the Great Commission, says "Go then and make disciples of all the nations"

This begins with those closest to us, in our own homes. I am learning that in my own family I need to fulfill the Great Commission, to make disciples. If 88% of those children raised in evangelical homes are leaving just as they are beginning life, something is wrong and I don't want it to happen in my home. If I cannot make disciples at home, how can I expect to make disciples anywhere else? One of the reasons the church exists is to equip the saints for the work of the ministry" This should happen naturally in the day to day of family members rubbing shoulders together in good times and bad.

God didn't have to create families, but He did –Genesis 1:28 says, "Be fruitful and multiply" He never takes this back. His mission and covenant is fulfilled thru families. His purpose for my family is for Mark and me to pass our faith to the next generation. Look at the Jews, from Abraham, then Isaac, Jacob, and finally twelve brothers came a whole nation to glorify God.

Psalm 78: 5-7states, "For He established a testimony in Jacob and appointed a law in Israel, commanding our fathers that they should make the great facts of God's dealings with Israel known to their children, that the generation to come might know them, that the children still to be born might arise and recount them to their children, that they night set their hope in God and not forget the works of God, but might keep His commandments"

Disciple making begins at home. If we can learn to get along and live in a loving fashion with each other at home, if we can learn to see God's principles for living together working out day by day, we can keep our children instead of losing 88% of them. Then when our children are grown and have gone through the disciple making process, they will be ready to step out into the world and begin the cycle all over in their families. People often laugh when I say I believe in biological evangelism but what better way to make disciples. I will probably not have opportunity to live with anyone else in such close proximity and be able to share my faith in such a day to day fashion.

On the other hand, we are all normal in our house and everyone has grumpy days and selfish days and there are certainly moments when we wonder if we have conveyed any truth to our children. Here are some things I try to remember throughout the day especially when life is crazy and everyone is grumpy.

My family is my church. Yes I worship in a bigger group on Sundays but my home is also a church. The Bible says "For wherever two or three are gathered in my name, there I Am in the midst of them". (Matt 18:20). The kingdom of God is in my kitchen, around my supper table and even in the group gathered to scrub the dishes. If I can see my home as a place of worship and fellowship and as a school of virtue I will have new vision for my role as a mother, or men, your role as a dad. We try to have family worship on a frequent basis. It's tough and sometimes gets drowned out by the cares of daily life. It requires constant refocusing of our priorities.

✴ In an article on family worship, J.W. Alexander said" the daily reading of God's holy Word by a parent before his children is one of the most powerful agencies of a Christian life. It is a constant dropping, but it wears its mark into the rock." ✴

My church needs to be a place of love and peace. I know this is easier said than done. We wrestle with it everyday at our house because we're human. How many of us come to church looking lovely and with nothing but good words in our mouth but at home we speak harshly to our children, or our husbands. The old song," They'll know we are Christians by our love" is expressed best in our homes. Or as someone else has said "by their fruit, you will know them" (Matt 7:20)

My domestic church must be a place of prayer. We try to establish some regular family times of prayer. Sometimes it's just a prayer of thanksgiving at every meal. Many or probably all of you already practice this. Pray together at the beginning of each day or if that's as chaotic as at my house, try a prayer together before the children head off to bed. Try a weekly devotion or Bible study. Let your children help plan it or present the study. Start small and don't be discouraged. Having regular devotions is one of the biggest struggles in our home .Its a spiritual battle. Keep at it.

I have to remember that my church has a mission. We are sent from our homes to be a light to those around us. There are people who are lonely, elderly, perhaps in mourning for a loss or have some other needs that we can help meet. These people are all around us. Mother Teresa said "Christ will sometimes come to us in these distressing disguises" The world is watching us. Matt 5:14 says "You are the light of the world. A city set on a hill cannot be hidden." And verse 16 states: "Let your light so shine before men that they may see your good deeds and glorify your Father who is in heaven." This requires us to open our hearts and homes to those in need.

In a seemingly hopeless culture, I try to encourage my children to have hope. There are days when I feel like selling everything and moving elsewhere and my children hear me mumbling over this but God has put me here and I can hope in His faithfulness and be a light where I am. There is no telling where this country is headed but this is not my final destination and I don't want my children to fear the trip.

I love Psalm 127: 4-5 where is says "As arrows are in the hand of a mighty man; so are children of the youth. Happy is the man that has his quiver full of them: they shall not be ashamed, but they shall speak with the enemies in the gate." It just struck me that I am not only building but training warriors who can speak with the enemies in the gate. What an awesome task. If I was in a town surrounded by enemies I think I would be afraid to go out and speak with them, but God wants me to raise children who are not ashamed to speak with the enemies. And in today's culture, we are surrounded by enemies. This thought drives me to spend more time in prayer for my family and gives me a renewed vision for training all these arrows.

If we look at the first century after Christ, life seemed pretty hopeless but studies have actually shown a growth rate of 40% per decade in the church. That seems to me pretty amazing. When I look at today's society all around me, it is so easy to get discouraged but God's power is unlimited and "He is not willing that any should perish". (II Peter 3:9) God's power has been changing people for centuries and it has not lost any strength. I want my children to believe in miracles and to believe that people can change. Lives and cultures can change and they can be a part of that change as they carry the good news of salvation with them wherever they go. There is hope for this century.

I need to teach my children to live by the teachings of the Church. Mark and I need to raise our homes up to the standards of Jesus Christ and his Church. It is a high standard, but the alternatives today are deadly. The early Christians did not convert the empire by compromising with the empire's ideas of family life. They did not compromise on divorce, contraception, abortion, infanticide, or homosexual activity. We need to hate sin and keep it far from our home but at the same time, love those who are sinners and reach those around us with the truth of Christ's love.

If I am sent by Christ to bring the gospel to the world and Mark is sent by Christ to bring the gospel to the world, then we need to disciple our children also and send them out to disciple the nations. My domestic church must preach this – life style evangelism.

Barbara Bush, in a speech to graduates summed it up "As important as your obligations as a doctor, lawyer, or business leader will be, you are a human being first, and those human connections- with spouses, with children, with friends- are the most important investments you will ever make. At the end of your life, you will never regret not having passed one more test, not winning one more verdict, or not closing one more deal. You will regret time not spent with a husband, a child, a friend, or a parent… Our success as a society depends not on what happens in the White House but on what happens inside your house."

Moms, let me encourage you. Whether you have one child or two children or ten or sixteen, we are all doing the same job. We are a huge part of this discipleship equation. Family discipleship has been described as a "life-long, time consuming, energy draining, painstaking path but worth every minute and every ounce of energy. Eternity hangs in the balance" (Author unknown)

There are days when this ideal seems just too big and I have to return again to read Galatians 6:9 where is says, "Do not become weary in well-doing…for in due season you will reap if you faint not." Mark and I can never do this job alone and we are far from finished, but God can do the job through us. Isaiah 58: 12 states, "Those from among you will rebuild the ancient ruins; you will rise up the age-old foundations; and you will be called the repairer of the breach, the restorer of the streets in which to dwell." This is the kind of building I am doing, not in my strength but with God's help.

Seth and Stephen, - the oldest and the youngest siblings

23.
A Vision for More

I got a call from a telemarketer a few years ago. She was fund-raising for a pro-life group. She began her spiel by asking me if I considered myself pro-life or pro-choice. I replied, "I'll let you guess. We have fourteen children and we're expecting one in July."

"Oh my," she said, "you must be pro-life. Fifteen children!" There was a long pause and then she said, " I'm not even going to ask you for money." And hung up.

One time my husband, Mark, overheard his father tell a waitress that he (Mark) was an "accident" I cannot believe that when I look at our sixteen lovely children. Psalm 139:16 says "You saw me before I was born and scheduled each day of my life before I began to breathe. Every day was recorded in your Book." (LB) That doesn't sound too accidental.

When we were first married, my father who is a physician convinced us that the responsible thing to do was to use birth control. After our first son was born we gave that up in favor of more "natural" methods. After five children were born in six years we decided that there was no more time, energy, finances or anything else to sustain this course we were on and so we must do something permanent. God intervened and a discussion with another couple (not about children at all, but about trusting God) brought us both independently to the same conclusion. We needed to let God decide how many children He had planned for us. Since then God has blessed us with eleven more children.

Many people we meet assume that we have so many children because we "have it all together?" Not at all (whatever "it" is). Most families today stop at two or perhaps three children. When we were expecting our fifth, life seemed a little bit out of control and we thought perhaps this was enough. God had other plans. Life is often chaotic and not nearly as organized as I would like it to be, but what is more important, perfect order or a few more blessings?

I also run into many people who make the comment "well you must have easy pregnancies or you wouldn't have all these children."

Not so. Our eighth baby required me to spend twelve weeks on my back lest I lose him because of an abnormal placenta. God graciously provided friends to help with the care of our other small children and we made it though. Since then there have been other pregnancies that seemed hard but I always say the end result is worth the effort.

Then there are always people we meet who say "of course you can have all these children, your financial situation is in order so it's easy for you"

Some years yes, and some no. Neither did God tell the Israelites in captivity in Egypt to stop multiplying just because they were slaves.

Through a number of circumstances, we came to the conclusion that we needed to trust God for the children He had for us. For two people raised in the generation we were, this was a novel idea and not always well received by those around us.

I came across a book a couple of years ago that challenged me to go a step further. It challenged me to ask myself if I would dare to ask God for more life. We ask Him to bless us in so many other ways but not in more children if we already have a couple. The name of the book? *Be Fruitful and Multiply* by Nancy Campbell. It is worth the read for every Christian couple. I'm no longer willing to say, each couple must decide what God has for them. This is a truth for all believers.

Just the other week, I found an old note dated 2006 where I asked God for another blessing, wrote it down and then stuck it in a book and forgot I wrote it. God didn't forget, however and several months later we discovered Stephen on the way. Now at the ripe old age of 48 I am challenged to ask God for another blessing. To see how that chapter ends, you will have to invest in the sequel to this book. God's first commandment is "be fruitful and multiply" (Genesis 1:28). He has never rescinded this that I can find in the Bible.

Malachi 2: 15 says God desires a godly seed from our marriage union. I am a strong proponent of biological evangelism. When God talks about blessing families with fruitfulness, he compares it to things that cannot be numbered, such as the sand on the beach or the stars in the sky. The blessing over Rebecca in preparation for her marriage was "Be thou the mother of thousands of millions" (Gen. 24:60)

In her book, Nancy Campbell also had this encouraging thought, "Parenting is the highest calling God has given to mankind. Every other career is subservient to this one. Everything else we do in life serves our highest calling of teaching and training the next generation for God."

As Christians, we should always be challenging our beliefs to see how they line up with God's thinking. We can't be neutral in this area. We should not despise this gift God has given us as women either. I have been challenged to see Motherhood as an eternal career. When a new baby is conceived in my womb, I have eternity in my womb. I will bring forth a life that will last forever and ever. What an awesome thought. Mark and I need to let God be sovereign. I have often wondered why it is more acceptable to die on the mission field serving Christ but if one was to die in childbirth, giving life to another, it is considered irresponsible. So what's the bottom line? It's not a matter of deciding how many children we should have or not have, but having a vision to bring forth a godly seed for God's glory.

I had a new thought last week: God has chosen to build His kingdom through the birth of more people. I don't mean just Christians, The only way any one can come into the kingdom of God requires a physical birth first, or at least conception. Satan has been murdering millions of children though abortion, and Christians protest this but he is just as active in Christian churches and homes tricking us into believing that we have the right and power to prevent conception. In doing this Satan is limiting the army of God and we are not even aware of it. Think about this, if the Christians in the last several generations hadn't made the choice to limit their families, how much more powerful God's army would be today. The numbers of babies who were not even conceived because of some of our practices is probably much greater than the number of babies aborted and yet birth control is a perfectly acceptable practice in the Church. I wonder if this makes the enemy laugh.

I wrote once, to a well known family oriented organization and asked why they didn't address the issue of Christians using birth control (note our control, not God's) and the reply I got back in a politely worded letter was that the issue is too controversial.

Last week a telemarketer called me and began asking me all sorts of questions about my stance on prolife/prochoice issues. I said, "Can I ask you a question? How do you feel about birth control?" I never imagined what a response I would get. She angrily replied" Don't preach to me" and

I think, would have hung up the phone on me if that was in her job code. I still haven't figured out how asking a simple question turned into preaching at her but her strong response helped me see again how Satan has tricked us into thinking we can decide to have children or not at our whim and have the audacity to think God doesn't care about this issue.

It's amazing how many people have asked why we have so many children. I expected that from people who are not Christians but so many in the Church seem to think this is an unusual idea.

As I get older, I am becoming more and more convinced that life is a gift and I do not want to be guilty of despising it. For all the abundance of scientific technology, only God gives life and only women have been ordained to bring forth that life. I am a life-giver. What an awesome thought. No president or king can compare with that and yet we have been tricked into believing that it is a curse and something only designed to tie us to our kitchen sinks. I had to learn to rethink many of the things I had been taught. I have been learning that it is an honor to bring a soul into the world that will live forever and then I have been given the opportunity to help disciple that new life with the vision of adding another soul to Christ's kingdom.

I am also becoming more aware that Satan deceives us with thoughts of careers outside the home and we have no time left to create and nurture life. Motherhood is a career that extends to eternity. No other career I could have chosen can do that. All these things will be left behind. I do not want to be empty of that which I could have taken into eternity – the redeemed souls of my children. Mark had a vision once about walking our family through a wall of fire. Everything we had attained in life was burned away except our children and that is what we came to God with. The enemy knows the power of life. Every person that comes into the world has the potential to glorify God with his life and to help destroy the works of the enemy. No wonder Satan is trying to destroy our desire to bear children and why he tries so hard to make us believe the sacrifice is too great. "The greatest threat to him (Satan) is a mother who understands her calling, to nurture and nourish life, to train, polish and sharpen these children for God's mighty purposes – and for the eternal age."(Nancy Campbell)

When I read that, I realized my weapons against Satan were my relationships with my husband and children and this also caused me to realize anew that I could not perform this task on my own. I need to spend time seeking God's help. One of my favorite hymns was written by Annie

J. Flint. It is taped to my cupboard door where I can read it whenever life gets overwhelming.

He giveth more grace as the burdens grow greater, He sendeth more strength as the labors increase; to added afflictions He addeth His mercy, to multiplied trials His multiplied peace.

When we have exhausted our store of endurance, when our strength has failed ere the day is half done, when we reach the end of our hoarded resources Our Father's full giving is only begun.

Fear not that thy need shall exceed His provision, Our God ever yearns His resources to share; Lean hard on the arm everlasting, availing; The Father both thee and thy load will up bear.

His love has no limits, His grace has no measure, His power has no boundary known unto men; for out of His infinite riches in Jesus He giveth, and giveth, and giveth again.

When I was 45 years old, I was pretty sure my child bearing years were over. After all, fifteen children were probably enough for any woman. Imagine my surprise when, on my 46 birthday I woke up to a strange nauseating feeling. I told myself I must have a touch of the local stomach bug but when my husband took me out for supper, I couldn't eat my favorite foods and began to feel a little suspicious. After several days, I finally went to the pharmacy to confirm my suspicions. Sure enough we were anticipating another arrival in the fall.

I believe life is a gift and meant to be celebrated and so even though my head told me that I was old and hadn't been pregnant for almost four years, and the baby clothes were probably all given away, not to mention maternity clothes, my heart said "Life is a gift from God" and I decided to do my best to embrace this experience wholeheartedly.

It is easy to celebrate life in our house. Just let fifteen children into the secret and a party begins. My oldest son was engaged and soon to be married. His response was "That's cool, mom, you'll be pregnant at my wedding" (So much for a flattering mother-of the groom dress)

Emmanuel, who was almost four, had a slightly different perspective: "Mom, you could have two babies, a boy for me and a girl for Jerusha to play with."

Ever since I passed the two children mark, well-meaning people have been making the comment "You must love being pregnant." Somehow they have confused the fact that being miserable for nine months has turned mysteriously into an enjoyable experience. How silly, but the truth is, the reward is worth the misery. How many people who panned for gold and actually found it said they wished they had never spent those days and night s shivering in Alaska looking. No, their reward was worth it.

Whatever you may believe about women and childbearing, the truth is still the truth. God designed us to have children. Its part of His plan and part of what makes us women, so once I got past the queasy feelings; I wanted to make the most of what could be my last pregnancy.

So, did this make the next eight months a bed of roses? Absolutely not. My brain hears the whispered thought "baby on the way" and I instantly gain ten pounds without even eating an extra bite. Then as this new one grows my legs ache, my back hurts, my husband tells me I'm sexier while I'm looking in the mirror saying "Yeah right, those watermelon seeds I swallowed have finally grown" and then there is labor. Contrary to popular belief, labor does not get easier each time you have another baby, especially since each time you are also older, but I focus on the reward at the end.

The greatest change I embraced was at the end of September when I could finally hold little Stephen, forget the past nine months and look forward with new excitement to what God's plan for Stephen is.

I have to continually focus myself on asking what is the big picture. Just as God has a plan for each of my children; He has a plan for my marriage and what it is producing.

I found that plan in the book of Malachi where God says marriage is for the purpose of producing a godly offspring (Malachi 2:15).

My Dad sent me an article a few weeks ago from the Dallas Morning News. The writer was discussing a sociologist named Carle Zimmerman whose book: *Family and Civilization* had just been republished.

One of Zimmerman's premises is that societies who are ruled by the loosening of constraints on individual members tend to have few or no children. They begin to focus on the pleasures of the present. He goes further to say that those cultures begin to make it difficult to sustain large families as well as costly, thus further decreasing the desire to have more children "History shows that when a culture ceases to value children above all, when traditional marriage and family structure is seen as merely an option, that culture will cease to have enough offspring to sustain itself.". While Zimmerman is not a religious man, he contends that the core problem here is a loss of faith. He points out that this happened in Greece, Rome and now is beginning to happen in our society.

His prediction is that those who survive will be those whose religious convictions lead them to have large families despite the cost.

Every now and then I wonder why I didn't make it to the mission field or do some other great thing and then God reminds me that I am doing something great even though I will never see the end result. I am a builder. He has entrusted Mark and I with all these children. How better to make disciples than with those who someone lives with day after day after day. This is the best opportunity God will ever give me to pass on my firm conviction that God has a plan for each of us I want to be extravagant for Jesus and leave a legacy of 100's of people who have the same vision of passing on the baton of faith so each generation after us (if Christ tarries) will increase the kingdom of God.

Mark and I have sixteen children. If God gives them each ten children, the next generation will have 160 children, but if the vision is passed along, my great grandchildren could number 1600 and the last generation I might live to see could number 160, 000. Imagine what an impact 160,000 more people could have in this world if they were all on fire for Christ. I hope I live to be 100.

Breinigsville, PA USA
21 March 2011
258110BV00001BA/29/P